Pray This Way
to Connect with God

D1640896

Pray This Way
to Connect with God

HAL GREEN

CASCADE *Books* · Eugene, Oregon

PRAY THIS WAY TO CONNECT WITH GOD

Cascade Books
An Imprint of Wipf and Stock Publishers
199 W. 8th Ave., Suite 3
Eugene, OR 97401

www.wipfandstock.com

PAPERBACK ISBN: 978-1-6667-4274-9
HARDCOVER ISBN: 978-1-6667-4275-6
EBOOK ISBN: 978-1-6667-4276-3

Cataloguing-in-Publication data:

Names: Green, Hal, author.

Title: Pray this way to connect with God / Hal Green.

Description: Eugene, OR: Cascade Books, 2022.

Identifiers: ISBN 978-1-6667-4274-9 (paperback) | ISBN 978-1-6667-4275-6 (hardcover) | ISBN 978-1-6667-4276-3 (ebook)

Subjects: LCSH: Prayer—Christianity.

Classification: BV 210.2 G735 2023 (paperback) |BV210.2 (ebook)

01/03/23

And whenever you pray, do not be like the hypocrites; for they love to stand and pray in the synagogues and at the street corners, so that they may be seen by others. Truly I tell you, they have received their reward. But whenever you pray, go into your room and shut the door and pray to your Father who is in secret; and your Father who sees in secret will reward you.

When you are praying, do not heap up empty phrases as the Gentiles do; for they think that they will be heard because of their many words. Do not be like them, for your Father knows what you need before you ask him.

Pray then in this way: . . .

(Matt 6:5–9a NRSV)

CONTENTS

BREATH PRAYERS

PRAYING THE SCRIPTURES

THE HEBREW BIBLE

THE NEW TESTAMENT

PRAYING WITH THE SAINTS

MEDITATIVE PRAYER

CONTEMPLATIVE PRAYER

AFTERWORD

PREFACE

GOD HAS BEEN THE center of my life since May 24, 1967. That was the day I first cried out for help to an unknown God. A twenty-four-year-old agnostic philosopher, on the way to becoming a psychologist, I suddenly realized that if there were no God, life had no firm foundation or meaning. This shuddering realization came about at a hotel bar in Salt Lake City, Utah. I had given a paper that Wednesday at the Rocky Mountain Psychological Association annual meeting; and I had just been offered a free ride for a PhD in counseling psychology at Colorado State University. Life was looking pretty good. Yet I felt something was wrong, something was missing. And not just something, but possibly the main something for my life.

Sitting there by myself at the bar, feeling unexpectedly empty, alone, and as if I were drifting aimlessly at sea, I took a couple of bar napkins and to my surprise, rapidly wrote the following to God, if there was a God:

> I've lost it, that little nexus that fosters both meaning and motivation.
> After wayfaring years, the circle is complete.
> I've met myself on snowy, stark mountain pass, going where I have been.
> I will not take that trip again, for I have learned its end.
> So I stop and pause and take no step.
> A tiny kernel, once failing to sprout, can neither rise nor return.
>
> A standstill.
> I want to succeed unaided, to break through the barren earth; but I cannot supply the needed nourishment.
> And so a plea is made:
> The hands upturned, strong legs forced to kneel, a desperate face skyward.
> With pride-smitten words I ask, "Help this 'modern man.'"

Then the question arose: how do you find God, if there is a God? As it would turn out, God has to find you. It used to be said that "a man chases a woman until she catches him." Just so, you can and perhaps must chase after God, until God finally catches you. Then you will discover that God had been secretly chasing after you long before you began your quest.

Four months later, on Friday, November 17, 1967, at a prayer meeting in the basement of a Catholic church in Des Moines, Iowa, God caught me, changing my life forever. I was then a student at Drake University, getting a master's degree in psychology. Through one of those seemingly chance meetings, I found out earlier that evening about a newly formed group of Drake students who were gathering in an effort to experience what was called the "baptism of the Holy Spirit." God blessed me with that life-changing baptism that very night.

From that night on, God and prayer have been at the center of my daily life. It has been a long and amazing journey. This is not, however, the time or place to tell you my story. That will require a memoir, hopefully on the way. What I want to tell you is this: If you now desire to know God, your desire is itself a gift of God, a hidden invitation for what will end up, sometime and somewhere, as a romantic relationship through and through. Your heart already knows this, whether or not it has let you know what it desires. It desires nothing less than union with the beloved.

It is most significant that on the very next Friday night, November 24, while meeting for a second time with the same group of newfound friends, in walked the woman who would become the love of my life. That means, on two successive Friday evenings, I met first the love of my eternal life, followed by the love of my temporal life.

I freely admit it: I am a romantic. I do not apologize for that; rather, I celebrate it. Being a romantic means that I lead with my heart. If not the first, my heart has the final say about my life. What that means spiritually is this: You let your heart guide you to the God who works especially in and through your heart. You will discover that as you draw nearer to God, to the God who is already nearer to you than you can imagine, your journey will become nothing short of a romantic "flight of the alone to the alone."

At the same time, I have been a seeker after truth. And a seeker after the ultimate good, the ultimate beauty, as well as the ultimate truth. At the highest level all three point to God. I discovered through direct experience that God is the most loving, lovable reality possible.

Take this truth to heart: When you seek God for God, rather than for this or that, and you do so with your whole heart, you will eventually encounter God. I cannot tell you how or when, but only that you will. Guaranteed. Your task is to persevere in your seeking; God's task, so to say, is in the finding. Through the prophet Jeremiah, God said, "When you search for me, you will find me; if you seek me with all your heart, I will let you find me, says the LORD" (Jer 29:13–14a). I found that to be the absolute truth.

This book will hopefully assist you in your seeking. And in your finding. It will focus on transforming prayer from a monologue with you addressing God, to prayer as a dialogue with God also addressing you. God is of course in sovereign charge of this process; yet God desires to commune with you far more than you do with God. As Kahlil Gibran said, "Strange, but as I drank of the Spirit, the Spirit drank of me." To that truth, which is very real to me, I can only add that the deeper you drink of the Spirit, the deeper the Spirit will drink of you. And as you give yourself to God, God will give God's self to you.

SCRIPTURE ABBREVIATIONS

HEBREW BIBLE / OLD TESTAMENT

Gen	Judg	Neh	Song	Hos	Nah
Exod	Ruth	Esth	Isa	Joel	Hab
Lev	1–2 Sam	Job	Jer	Amos	Zeph
Num	1–2 Kgs	Ps (pl. Pss)	Lam	Obad	Hag
Deut	1–2 Chr	Prov	Ezek	Jonah	Zech
Josh	Ezra	Eccl (or Qoh)	Dan	Mic	Mal

NEW TESTAMENT

Matt	Acts	Eph	1–2 Tim	Heb	1–2–3 John
Mark	Rom	Phil	Titus	Jas	Jude
Luke	1–2 Cor	Col	Phlm	1–2 Pet	Rev
John		Gal		1–2 Thess	

INTRODUCTION: HOW TO READ AND PRAY THIS BOOK

GOD IS THE HIDDEN teacher of prayer. All you need to bring for prayer is yourself and your desire to know God personally, directly. If you do not have that desire, then this book is not for you, at least not at the present moment of your life. The thing is, you do not know what tomorrow may bring, and the closer you get to life's inevitable end, the greater will be your desire to know what or who may be on the other side. Thus, religion has been defined as our "ultimate concern." That means "ultimate" in two senses: what matters most today, the ground on which you stand; and what matters most as you draw near to the "event horizon" of the black hole called death. As you will hopefully discover, if you have not already, there is no ground as powerful, unshakable, and enduring as that of God, our one true "ground of being."

The seeking of God for God's self is of course not the only form of prayer, but it is the most important. Granted, we all pray for the safety and well-being of ourselves, our family, and loved ones. We also pray for those in need, from our neighbors to our nation, from our environment to the world, as well as doing what we can to make a difference. We pray about our fears and hopes and desires for differing outcomes. Prayers about these concerns will definitely be addressed in the prayer exercises that follow. Yet my major thrust throughout will be on *turning a prayer monologue into a prayer dialogue with God.*

I ask that you begin this "how to pray" book with the prayers themselves, rather than the section "About Prayer." I do not want you to get bogged down with prayer principles and issues. Rather, I would like you to get into the prayers right away. You can read through the sections detailing various aspects of prayer later, once you have begun praying the prayers themselves.

Praying to God over time is a bit like journeying around an immense stand-alone mountain, so high that clouds perpetually shroud the top. While the mountain may not change, your position and point of viewing will alter as you continue walking. It is rightly said that when one person changes in a relationship, the relationship changes as well. That means that what prayer or kind of prayer works for you now may not be as good a fit later; conversely, what seems not to speak to you now, may speak to you later. If a particular prayer addresses you where you are right now, then let it speak to you. Stay with it for a while. Perhaps another prayer that does not address you now, may well address you later on in your destined journey to God.

This is a progressive or growth book. I begin with simple yet effective breath prayers, then move on to praying the Scriptures, followed by praying with the saints. Next will come meditative prayer; and lastly, contemplative prayer. The final section is for those who are prepared to go deeper into prayer, those who seek conscious connection with God. I was not always ready for contemplative prayer. But when my desire for God reached critical mass, I discovered the prayer encounters of medieval Christian mystics. These saints may seem out of style now, since we have been stuck in a "scientific mindset" for the last two hundred years. But the time is coming, and may now be here, when what Fr. Karl Rahner prophesied will prove true: "The Christian of the future will be a mystic, or will not exist at all."

Everything is at stake in the long overdue return to the focus on knowing God directly. Such knowledge permeated the medieval mystic saints. I hope this book will be of assistance to those who seek an immediate encounter with the ultimate beauty, goodness, and truth: God.

I have lived and prayed through the contents which follow. And again I say, if you seek God with all your heart, you will definitely find God (see Jer 29:13–14). In fact, you cannot seek God unless God already seeks you. Your desire is itself God's invitation, engraved upon your heart. Trust that invitation and let your heart lead you to God. It alone knows the way. Your prayer journey will be the most profound passage of and through your life.

ABOUT PRAYER

"For me, prayer is a surge of the heart; it is a simple look turned toward heaven, it is a cry of recognition and of love, embracing both trial and joy."

—Thérèse de Lisieux

"Prayer is the soul's sincere desire. Your desire is your prayer. It comes out of your deepest needs and it reveals the things you want in life."

—Joseph Murphy

"Go where your best prayers take you."

—Frederick Buechner

WHAT PRAYER IS

PRAYER IS COMMUNICATION WITH God in all its forms. This includes intimate as well as seemingly distant communication, from monologues to dialogues, from texts to touch, from speech to silent communion. Prayer establishes the bridge between God and humanity. It is as vital to our personal well-being to develop a flourishing prayer life, as it is to learn how to communicate love to human loved ones.

An analogy may be helpful here. There are two sides or hemispheres to the human brain. What connects them, so that they can communicate with each other, and work together for that person to be whole and healthy, is a band of neural fibers called the "corpus callosum." If this band is damaged or destroyed, that person can no longer function fully as themselves.

To extend the analogy: let the left hemisphere represent our embodied being connected to the physical universe. And let the right hemisphere represent our spiritual being connected to the unseen kingdom of God. That means we have a "joint citizenship" in both this cosmos and heaven. This was already understood by St. Augustine back in the fifth century.

Here is the deal: *we are meant to live in both hemispheres at the same time.* Call the spiritual domain a "parallel universe," or perhaps an undiscovered dimension of a "multiverse." It is at least as vast as the physical universe. When you pray through this spiritual "corpus callosum" that exists invisibly between you and God, you enter into this "other side," which at the same time enters into you. You come from and belong to this spiritual hemisphere of heaven, and when you cease to exist in the physical universe, you will find yourself in this, your true home. As Augustine prayed, "Our hearts are restless until they find rest in You." That means in God and God's dominion.

Finally, it is important to note that in the current view of physics, the physical cosmos consists of 68 percent dark energy, 27 percent dark matter, and only 5 percent physical, observable matter. That means physical space is not empty; nor is spiritual space, even if, like the physical universe, it is mostly invisible—here anyway. In short, the space between you and God is not empty. The only way to discover this is through prayer. The state of your prayer life *is* the state of your relationship with God.

My purpose in these prayer exercises is to assist you to enter more fully into a daily dialogue with God across the connective fibers of prayer. That includes entering into the spiritual kingdom of God, while consenting to God's entrance into you. May you discover the astounding things God can do for you even in brief prayers.

HOW TO PRAY

As you have an inborn capacity for language, so you have an inborn capacity for prayer. And just as you develop language skill through dialogue with your family of origin, so you develop prayer facility through dialogue with God. One difference between human and divine communication: God knows what is in your heart and mind before you do. Thus, you may need to pray to discover what is in your heart, seeking expression. And you must pray as you can, not as you cannot. Above all, be honest with God, who will never criticize you for being honest; rather you will find God ever gracious and merciful, kind and understanding.

The good news is that God will teach you how to pray. The apostle Paul said: "Likewise the Spirit helps us in our weakness; for we do not know how to pray as we ought, but that very Spirit intercedes with sighs too deep for words. And God, who searches the heart, knows what is the mind of the Spirit, because the Spirit intercedes for the saints according to the will of God" (Rom 8:26–27).

Also, trust in the prayer instruction of Jesus: "But whenever you pray, go into your room and shut the door and pray to your Father who is in secret; and your Father who sees in secret will reward you. When you are praying, do not heap up empty phrases as the Gentiles do; for they think that they will be heard because of their many words. Do not be like them, for your Father knows what you need before you ask him" (Matt 6:6–8).

Speak whatever is in your heart. Let your heart guide you, for it secretly knows the way to God as well as the deepest content of your desired message to God. Let your words and sentiments surface without fear; for again, the God who loves you already knows what is in you, yet still loves you. It is you who must learn how to pray through prayer itself.

I will be offering you a multitude of brief prayer exercises. They will include classical language and techniques of prayer, such as breath prayers, praying the Scriptures, and praying with the saints. But since prayer is really your relationship with God, do not feel confined by these prayers. Simply let your heart's naked desire guide you to God's heart. Take on faith that God seeks you far more than you seek God. And as Jesus said, no one can snatch one of God's own from God (John 10:2). There is no lost, but only found with God.

Sit comfortably in a straight-back chair, with both feet on the ground and hands on your thighs. Close your eyes—unless you prefer to keep your eyes open. Hopefully these prayer exercises will lead to the calming sense of God's presence with and in you. As you are able, let your prayer period lengthen to perhaps twenty minutes, twice a day if possible. But then, that is really between you and God. Prayer represents the greatest of all adventures, as well as an advance foray into your final destiny: the heaven of pure, perpetual, mutual life with God.

THE KINDS OF PRAYER

As THERE ARE DIFFERENT kinds of communication, so also are there different kinds of prayer, moving in differing directions. Here I offer ten interwoven kinds of prayer. In the actual practice of prayer, however, one mode easily extends into another. Truly, during a single prayer period, you can interweave all ten forms. We see this operative in the biblical book of Psalms, where the psalmist may move rapidly from thanksgiving to lament, from intercession to praise. Some types of prayer are soliloquies, without expecting or anticipating a response from God other than listening. The hope here is on the aftermath of the prayer, that the action prayed for from God will come about.

Other modes of prayer seek above all the presence of God. That means, they desire *dialogue*, direct connection with God, like Elijah seeking God on Mount Carmel (1 Kgs 19:9–18). The intensity of desire here is for God, which no one other than God can satisfy. Such desire is one of God's greatest gifts, which will ultimately lead to union with God.

Here are ten categories of prayer, with examples from the Psalms:

1. Adoration/awe/love/reverence/worship: *I love the LORD, because he has heard my voice and my supplications. Because he inclined his ear to me, therefore I will call on him as long as I live* (116:1–2).

2. Thanksgiving/praise/gratitude: *I am your servant; I am your servant, the child of your serving girl. You have loosed my bonds. I will offer to you a thanksgiving sacrifice and call on the name of the LORD* (116:16–17).

3. Lament/complaint/cry for assistance: *Do not forsake me, O LORD; O my God, do not be far from me; make haste to help me, O LORD, my salvation* (38:21–22).

4. Confession/contrition/regret/forgiveness: *Have mercy on me, O God, according to your steadfast love; according to your abundant mercy blot out my transgressions. Wash me thoroughly from my iniquity, and*

cleanse me from my sin. For I know my transgressions, and my sin is ever before me (51:1–3).

5. Intercession/petition/prayer for others: *Help us, O God of our salvation, for the glory of your name; deliver us, and forgive our sins, for your name's sake* (79:9).

6. Healing/well-being/hope: *Be gracious to me, O Lord, for I am languishing; O Lord, heal me, for my bones are shaking with terror . . . Turn, O Lord, save my life; deliver me for the sake of your steadfast love* (6:2, 4).

7. Guidance/discernment/wisdom: *You guide me with your counsel, and afterward you will receive me with honor* (73:24).

8. Protection/safety: *You who live in the shelter of the Most High, who abide in the shadow of the Almighty, will say to the Lord, "My refuge and my fortress; my God, in whom I trust"* (91:1–2).

9. Comfort/assurance/peace: *Even though I walk through the darkest valley, I fear no evil; for you are with me; your rod and your staff—they comfort me* (23:4).

10. Presence/knowledge of/naked desire for God: *Whom have I in heaven but you? And there is nothing on earth that I desire other than you. My flesh and my heart may fail, but God is the strength of my heart and my portion forever* (73:25–26).

The central focus of the prayer exercises in this book will be on generating a dialogue with God. That means encountering God directly, person to Person. The greatest spiritual need of our time is for a renewal of the knowledge of God. As in the time of the prophet Hosea, there is "no knowledge of God in the land" (Hos 4:1). The only way to attain such knowledge is through prayer. And it must be prayer build on a desire for God, for direct knowledge, something for which you yourself must pray.

THE WHY OF PRAYER

ONE OF THE MOST significant and often repeated questions is, "Why pray?" What is the purpose of prayer? What are you supposed to get out of it? Here are four goals of prayer:

1. *Self-discovery*: What do you seek? How strongly do you seek it? How long have you sought it? You can learn a great deal about yourself and who you really are by examining your history of prayers to God. Though God knows our thoughts and needs before we do (Ps 139:4; Matt 6:8), you still have to voice them. It is essential to your well-being to let your desires, your hopes as well as your fears, become words. As a therapist, I would tell my clients that all we had available to assist us in their healing process are words. Then I would add that we *are* word; our personal creation began when God mystically addressed us into being, saying in effect: "Let there be, you!" Therefore, we do not just *have* language; we *are* language, the language of God. Yet if we do not speak what is in our hearts, how will we know what is really bothering us, what we truly desire as well as fear? The Psalms well demonstrate that God has given us permission to say whatever is on our heart and mind. We just need to keep on praying until we gain a sense of having said and maybe discovered what is going on within us.

2. *Self-transformation*: "Thy will be done," said Jesus in the garden of Gethsemane before his arrest (Matt 26:42 KJV). One of my seminary professors often prayed while walking outside in the early evening, off and away from other persons. Though he did not usually say anything out loud, there was nonetheless a lot going on in him. He said that at the beginning of his prayer, he typically had some problematic issue he wanted to present to God. Here, the prayer might begin in an apparently oppositional manner, like many of the Psalms, e.g., "My God, my God, why have you forsaken me? Why are you so far from helping me, from the words of my groaning? O my God, I cry by day, but you do

9

not answer; and by night, but find no rest" (Ps 22:1–2). Yet if he persevered in prayer sufficiently while walking in the quiet darkness, he said that he would usually find himself now appositionally with God and God with him, as in "me and God against the world."

3. *God-appeal*: We simply cannot help but ask, even beg God for what we seek God to do for us. Can we ever get God to change God's mind, so to say? God did when Moses entreated God to relent from punishing Israel (Exod 32:10–14). And even more importantly, Jesus tells us to persevere in prayer, in beseeching God to answer us in an affirming way (Luke 18:1–8).

   Many years ago, I asked God to help me find a golf ball I had just hit into the woods. Then I felt stupid, asking the high and holy God for a mere golf ball. Feeling like an embarrassed child, I apologized to God and withdrew my request. Yet at once God unexpectedly spoke telepathically to me: "Don't you tell me what is important! If you want something, ask for it!"

   Mind you, that does not mean you will get it! But if something is on your heart, lift the words of your heart to God, from whom all words come, and unto whom all words will return.

4. *God-encounter*: This is the most important "why" of prayer. Here the only desire is to encounter God, leading toward not just a temporary communion, but ultimate union after this life. Prayer is simply the only means available to open us sufficiently to receive the pure gift of God's presence.

DISCOVERING YOUR PRAYER PATH

You HAVE YOUR OWN prayer path to God. You just have to discover it, and learn to traverse it, slowly, over time, rather like walking a labyrinth. The end is assured, as long as you keep on walking, moving forward, and trusting God, especially when your life seems to be moving at odds with your hoped-for destined end in God.

Your thought process will not gain you entrance into the relationship with God, which is your destiny. It is your heart that must lead you. Your heart knows the way *to* as well *of* God, though initially more unconscious than conscious in you. You have to invite what is within you to surface in your consciousness, whether alone or with another assisting you. You must learn how to listen and respond. The way was already imprinted on your heart by God at the moment of your spiritual birth through God's address, which preceded your physical embodiment here.

Try though you may, there is only one way to God for you, one narrow gate wide enough just for you, through which your heart will guide you. I cannot say this too often: the key to the opening of heaven to you resides in the desire of your heart, restless until it finally attains union with God— which is your one true home.

Your path begins with a desire, a hunger and thirst that nothing will satisfy for long. The prompting of your heart will always be for "something more," "something else." The truth, which may take you decades to finally realize, is *nothing in this temporary abode will satisfy the deeper longing of your being.* You were created by God, for God.

From your desire must come next a listening, not yet a movement toward what you are not sure you know or even believe might actually exist and be available to you.

After listening you will have to decide whether to risk moving toward the deepest desire of your heart, "faithing" that satisfaction may somehow, somewhere, sometime be found. Then begins the search. What you will likely not grasp at first is that there are two sides to this search: God is seeking you far more than you are seeking God. In fact, you cannot thirst for the living water of God without God having already put that thirst in you, as a summons for communion, leading to union. As Jesus said: "You did not choose me but I chose you. And I appointed you to go and bear fruit, fruit that will last, so that the Father will give you whatever you ask him in my name" (John 15:16). God is the hidden initiator of prayer, and we merely the responders.

Trust that your prayer path will become clear as you move through it on your way to the God who is silently calling you.

YOUR PRAYER LANGUAGE

REGARDLESS OF WHAT LANGUAGE you may speak to those around you, when you pray, you will pray in your native tongue. Why? Because that is the language not only of your birth, but also of your heart. And it is your heart that must always lead in prayer. It is to your heart that God will respond directly. Prayer, like love, arises as a mystery of the heart. As Blaise Pascal famously said, "The heart has its reasons, which reason known not of."

It is best to learn how to pray by praying the prayers of others, beginning with the biblical psalms. Let the great prayers of others, including the saints, help direct your feelings, hopes, and desires down the historic river bank-like channels that can lead you to the ocean of God. Like the language of the Bible, these prayers are timeless, and address multiple situations.

Yet we are all timed beings. And though you may and must start with these prayers, which will doubtless put words to your inner being, you will also eventually have to put your prayers into your own words, addressing your specific situations. For prayer always brings us fully into the present moment between God and us. It is as personal as we ever get. Learning how to pray in your own language is akin to the time-honored process of learning how to paint. You begin by copying the masters; and in time, you discover what speaks for and what does not speak for you and your heart. Truth is, God will be right in the middle of this process, though unseen and undetected. For it is God who teaches us how to pray (see Rom 8:26–27).

These prayer exercises are designed to assist you in putting into words what you seek of and from God. As you meditate and reflect on this or that phrase, feel free to paraphrase what is there by putting its meaning into your own words. It would be good to record them in a notebook. Over time, your paraphrases will form a sonar-like outline of your heart and soul, your longings, fears, and hopes. They then can become the content of your continuing prayer. And you may slowly discern God's actions in response to your prayer. Even should that response be decades away, even should you have forgotten the wish that God nevertheless remembered. So that when it finally arrives, God will revive your memory of asking.

Through this process, you will discover the central themes of your relationship with God. Hopefully you will realize the importance of persevering in praying for what you seek, just like that widow whom Jesus praised (Luke 18:1–8). Such protracted prayers shape and strengthen your character before God.

WHAT TO PRAY

WHEN YOU ARE WANTING and ready to pray, the next issue is what to pray. By now you have probably figured out the best answer: *pray whatever is in your heart*. Let your heart—without any fear whatsoever—approach the heart of God. And yes, God does have a heart. Biblical passages make that clear. Three examples: God's heart grieves (Gen 6:6); God's heart recoils at the idea of coming with wrath (Hos 11:8); and Jesus says he is "gentle and humble in heart" (Matt 11:29).

God knows what is in your heart, long before you do. And God loves you, due to God's ever mysterious, yet ever consistent, unchanging nature. So you may as well give words to what is within you seeking to be spoken and released. This will include prayers for others as well as for yourself. Above all, as you give words to the depths of your heart, you will discover your desire for God, which surprisingly is the strongest and most determined longing of your inner being. Yet you may have to get through many other prayer pleas to discover this amazing fact: you actually seek God for God, as you would seek "the one" in romantic love terms.

The prayers in this book seek to give you permission, direction, and words. Hopefully you will find yourself able to pray these prayers, able to move into their gentle currents and find yourself at home and comforted. "Comforted" means strengthened as well as supported.

Hopefully, on the basis of my prayer offerings to you, you will discover where you are spiritually, and what you want to say to God, and have God say to you, or do for or with or in you. Treat the prayers presented here as runways to get the wings of your soul aloft. Once aloft, you can change your course whenever you like. But at least you will be airborne in the heightened atmosphere of God's Spirit. At that point, you will experience the absolute freedom of prayer.

God's gracious permission is for you to say and seek whatever you will. Discovering what is in you is as great an adventure as discovering what—or who—is around and before you.

If and when you like, you can write your own prayers, or paraphrase any of the prayers offered here. That way, you can make them more fully your own. Remember that your prayer is strictly between you and God, and that God knows what you want to say before you do. As you seek to make prayer your own, be gratefully aware that God seeks to make you God's own.

THE BENEFITS OF PRAYER

PRAYER ESTABLISHES YOUR PERSONAL, private relationship with God. It is the greatest love relationship you will ever have; it may begin here, but it will not end here. Amazingly, it is eternal. When you pray, the hidden God will be gazing on you from eternity, and seeing not only where you are, but where God wants you to be. God seeks what is best for you not only for the moment, but for eternity. Your task is to let God be God, and to seek above all to do God's will, even if you do not understand the "whys." Trust that God does. And that there will be an answer.

Nevertheless, you cannot help but to approach God with your own expectations and agenda, which you ask God to meet and carry out. God understands that, and will not criticize you for any heart request. Risk believing in Jesus' words: "Your Father knows what you need before you ask him" (Matt 6:8). Believe also that whenever you turn to God in prayer, you will be heard, regardless of whether you feel that you have been.

There are immediate and long-term benefits of prayer. The immediate benefit comes from inviting God into your life, for as the ancient rabbis said, *God is wherever we let God in*. The subsequent benefits or fruit of prayer are essentially those which arise from the presence of the invited Spirit: "love, joy, peace, patience, kindness, generosity, faithfulness, gentleness, and self-control" (Gal 5:22–23). And like growing fruit in a garden, it takes time, good soil, sun, warmth, and rain. And different fruit have different patterns and periods of growth.

Disciplined prayer is akin to disciplined exercise. You cannot expect too much too quickly when you begin to weight train. It takes time and commitment to strengthen your body. Just so, it takes time and commitment to strengthen your relationship to God. My single desire when I leave a gym after a workout is to feel better than I did when I first entered. The same goes for prayer: I want to end a prayer period feeling better than when I began it. If nothing else, I have addressed God and expressed where I am: I have put words and my heart before the Holy One, who is always listening, and who will respond in God's timing and way. Above all, I hope I will have sensed the Beloved with me and in me, and that our dialogue continues.

Do not, however, rely on your feelings, or on the apparent effects of prayer on your soul and life. I remember a man did not think anything was happening while engaging in daily centering prayer. So he considered quitting it. Yet his family protested: "No! Do not stop! You are much easier to be around." Thus, and most importantly, the benefits of prayer include its positive effects on those around you.

HOW GOD SPEAKS
TO US IN PRAYER

GOD CAN GET THROUGH to us what God wants to get through, at any time. You can of course seem to close off from God, or turn away in disbelief, anger, or despair. Yet if God wants to get your attention, God will. That being said, it is important to understand how God communicates with us during prayer, usually in subtle and unexpected ways.

There are *seven essential entryways* in us through which God may stealthily make God's presence and will known during prayer. The better you understand these, the more readily your apparent prayer *monologue* can be grasped as an actual prayer *dialogue*, as something "with" rather than "to" God. It is vital to patiently wait upon, and listen for the Lord around these entryways. And also to take on faith that God addresses you daily, in a variety of elusive ways, though most importantly in prayer.

God's entryways in prayer include:

1. *Thoughts*. You may find yourself thinking in a new, anointed way, indicating God at work. Most every morning during my prayer time, God gives me insights and directions for my writing.

2. *Imagination*. You may discover yourself imagining something that God authors. This is like a daydream you did not seem to start, which reveals something God wants you to realize.

3. *Will*. You may discover new desires, a greater will or passion for God and service. It may prove necessary to ask God to affect your will directly, so it may be in accord with God's will. If so, pray and then get out of God's way.

4. *Feelings*. Your feelings may change; dark ones dissipate, while bright ones dawn. God can gently ease your burdens and cleanse your heart.

5. *Memory.* You may find yourself remembering past moments when God was there for you. If God was there for you yesterday, God will assuredly be with you today. Trust God.

6. *Intuition.* The sixth sense. This is the underappreciated means of direct discernment, and how you can tell the "who" of persons. Through intuition, you can sense the presence and person of God, in ways which can neither be proven nor denied. Discernment is also how you can distinguish what is of God, of yourself, or of the evil one.

7. *Speech to the heart.* The ancient monks describe listening to God with the "ear of your heart." God can and does, albeit infrequently and always unexpectedly, address you, typically with very few words and little emotion. God does so through what the rabbis termed the "voiceless echo." These words will always be what you need to hear, and always for your good and eternal well-being.

HOW TO TELL IF A
WORD IS FROM GOD

You may on occasion have a vivid sense during prayer that God has given you a "word of the Lord." You will likely hear it as a "voiceless echo." Whether alone or more often in a group, it needs to be shared and tested. The apostle John said we needed to test every spirit to see whether it is from God (1 John 4:1). When I have received a "word of the Lord," mostly in a prayer group, I have shared it with the group right away. And I have left it for the group to confirm. If I am alone, I test it out with spiritual friends and fellow clergy.

The question remains, how can you be reasonably sure that such a word is from God? It will have the following elements: *It is clear, distinct, and just what you need to hear. You do not forget it; nor does its impact diminish over time. It gives you peace and brings you greater wholeness; it contains mercy and grace. It strengthens and ignites your heart, drawing you closer to God. It does not contradict but is supported by Scripture and tradition. You are always grateful to have heard it, if for no other reason than it attests to God's ongoing presence with and working in you.*

We witness these elements at Jesus' baptism, when God said, "This is my Son, the beloved, with whom I am well pleased" (Matt 3:15). We also witness these elements when Christ strengthened a beleaguered Paul by saying, "My grace is sufficient for you, for [my] power is made perfect in [your] weakness" (2 Cor 12:9).

God's telepathic words are generally *understated, brief, and concise; yet they penetrate directly to the heart.* They tend not to be overly dramatic or intensified by some external display; hence, *they do not rob you of your freedom; they do not diminish your ability to say yes or no to God.* God could seem more casual than you might want, considering how decisive God's message can be for your life. Yet God's calm, gentle approach affords you some time and space to respond.

God can of course address you in dramatic fashion, replete with dynamic signs. Christ did that to Saul on the road to Damascus, with blinding light accompanying his word of revelatory warning: "Saul, Saul, why do you persecute me?" (Acts 9:4). And on rare occasions, God can address you decisively; God has done so to me, when as a pastor I needed to see, be with, and pray for someone *right away*. This was usually when someone was dying or in serious crisis.

God will address you through one or more of these seven means: *nature, natural events, supernatural events, Scripture, other persons, the direct inner witness of prayer, and in sleeping dreams.* God desires that you hear, believe in, trust, and act on what God is saying. *God speaks forgiveness and healing to your past; God speaks faith and love to your present; God speaks hope and promise to your future.* God's address, then, is meant to heal your yesterday, satisfy the neediness of your today, and rekindle your heart with new possibilities for your tomorrow.

THE CIRCLE OF PRAYER

PRAYER MOVES IN A continuous circle, from God to you, then from you to God. You will never know for sure who actually began a specific period of prayer. What you feel in your heart that impelled you to pray may have been proceeded by the secret prompting of God.

Yet prayer, like language itself, truly begins in God, streams from the word, which flows eternally between the beloved and the lover, right along with the love itself. Prayers, like love songs, are generated in the unseen, gravity-like field of Spirit between you and the beloved, God. Thus, melodies and prayers represent mutual life, the holy "rubbing" of your soul over against God's Spirit. Prayer, like music, does not merely flow through us: it also arouses us, plays with us, interacts with us such that the prayer event itself can change us, as well as the prayer content. The Psalms are replete with examples of the psalmist starting at one place in the opening verses of the psalm, and ending in an entirely different, typically better place by the end.

In short, God secretly acts upon your heart and soul as you pray, to turn you from fear to trust, pain to peace, doubt to faith. As Paul grasped: "for it is God who is at work in you, enabling you both to will and to work for his good pleasure" (Phil 2:13). So if you stay in a prayer long enough, and give God permission, God will likely change your heart to be in accord with God's will.

Prayer often has an overt and covert content, a reason you start with, and what surfaces and affects the content and direction the prayer eventually follows. In a similar way, time and again while conducting a counseling session, where we began slowly morphs into other subjects, ever closer to the heart of the matter, to why that person is really there, and to what is actually at stake at this moment of their lives. And imagine this: our amazingly patient God knows all this before we even start down the linguistic path. The patience of God is beyond our grasp.

Put differently, prayer knows where it is going, even if you do not, at least until the prayer has come full circle. Remember that you *are* word, rather than merely *having* words. God created you by addressing you into being: "Let there be, you!" I believe that somewhere in your unconscious is the memory of that address, along with who God is and the "who" God is calling you to be.

Being word, your prayer words must open and remain open to God like flower petals to the sun. And let there be silent pauses between words, to enhance your grasp of what you are saying and to whom you are speaking. Words both establish and reveal relationships, including between God and you.

PRAYER EXPECTATIONS

IT IS IMPORTANT TO be aware of your expectations about prayer. It is also important to beware of them. We all have expectations about many things, from the weather to the behavior of loved ones. Much of our daily life is preceded by and lived through the prism of, and evaluated by, our expectations. It has been said that "relationships go awry when you either don't get what you expected, or what you get, you did not expect."

This is also true regarding your relationship with God. And therefore, your prayer life. As you have an attitude toward God, so you also develop positive and negative expectations regarding what might happen during and as a consequence of prayer. Speaking for myself, it is easy to set the bar either too high or too low regarding what I expect from this or that prayer. But I will never forget a "word of the Lord" to me back in 1980, when I was getting doubtful and depressed about the apparent direction my life was taking. I don't think I was even praying, but here came God's "voiceless echo": "Expect less, accept more." Now that does not mean to give up your expectations regarding what you want out of life; rather, it means to focus more on acceptance and appreciation of what you actually have, than for what you do not and want. As psychologist Abraham Maslow said, "We tend to undervalue what we have, and overvalue what we do not have."

Approach prayer with *faith, hope, perseverance,* and *acceptance.* Hold on tightly to all four of these. Focus on your faith in even asking, rather than your doubts. If God seems not to be answering your prayer, at least not the way you want, then do not lose hope—which must always be in God, rather than specific outcomes. And do as Jesus told us: "Pray always and not to lose heart" (Luke 18:1). Show God through your perseverance what is really important to you. And finally, all prayer must conclude with acceptance, with, "if this be in accordance with Your will . . . Thy will be done" (Matt 26:42 KJV).

Do you have unanswered questions about prayer? I sure do. And I intend to respectfully ask God to answer them, when I get to the other side, at least to the extent that I can understand God's answers.

I have prayed for and with persons across four decades. I have witnessed healing miracles, and also sad endings. But one thing I absolutely will not do is to give up on God or on prayer. Pushing aside expectations, I press on to pray for God to be God manifestly among us. And I believe that, as the Beatles song put it, "there will be an answer, let it be."

PRAYER DISTRACTIONS

WHENEVER YOU PRAY, THERE are bound to be distractions of one kind or another. Accept that and adjust to it. That is one of the reasons why the prayers I offer you are designed to be brief. It is easier to let go of other concerns and stay focused on God for five or ten minutes than for thirty. You have to work up to the latter by practicing the former.

Realize that your mind never stops thinking, even during all five of the stages of sleep. Don't fight yourself; rather, work calmly with yourself. Treat your consciousness more like a child than an adult; instead of insisting: "Don't go there!," say rather, "You do not have to go there; you can go here." Do not fear anything in yourself; rather, love all that you are, the unknown as well as the known. Listen to yourself as you would your best friend. Take on faith that God is in you, as well as with you. Trust that God will teach you how to pray, and help you to gently overcome distractions. Grant God permission to do just that.

How can you accomplish this? By letting your consciousness go, to flow continuously like a river with its own current. Choose to sink silently below the surface current where everything slows down to stillness; image yourself like a diver in a comfortable oxygenated suit. Boats of this or that concern will float above you, driven by the current of your consciousness. They will seek your attention. The good news is that you have the God-given freedom to let them pass you by. And if one should capture your attention, and you find yourself on deck, simply reenter the quiet waters of prayer by gently turning your attention back to God.

The key to prayer attention resides in your will. What your heart desires is more resolute than the short-term needs of your body. The question is, do you really *want* to connect with God? God says that if you seek God with your whole heart, God will let you find God (Jer 29:13–14). Yet if you are not really hungry, you may merely play with food. As is said, "hunger is the best sauce." So also is the desire for God.

When it comes to prayer, don't trust your feelings. Even if you feel nothing is happening, trust that, "it is God who is at work in you, enabling you both to will and to work for his good pleasure" (Phil 2:13). Your soul is like an iceberg: only about one-third is above the surface waters of consciousness. The other two-thirds remain below your awareness, until you are ready to know and embrace what God has been preparing in your unconscious.

If you are really interested in listening to and for someone, say a loved one sitting across from you at a busy restaurant, you will strive to listen to what that person is saying with your whole being. God is truly that beloved one, who is always before you as the "eternal You" of your life, and not just for now, but forever. God deserves nothing less than your whole being.

PRAYER STATES

WHEN YOU PRAY, SEEK to enter into a "prayer state." To best understand what prayer states are, I offer two examples. First, concerning brain waves. Five electrical brain waves have been determined. They are, from the slowest deep sleep to the fastest frequency while processing information: delta, theta, alpha, beta, and gamma. Alpha is in the middle, and occurs when you are daydreaming, meditating, or praying, and are relaxed and calm. You can also enter into alpha through deep breathing. When you are fully awake and resting in the moment, you are in alpha.

The second example has to do with the difference between a monologue and a dialogue. To again refer to Jesus' instruction on prayer: "But whenever you pray, go into your room and shut the door and pray to your Father who is in secret; and your Father who sees in secret will reward you. When you are praying, do not heap up empty phrases as the Gentiles do; for they think that they will be heard because of their many words. Do not be like them, for your Father knows what you need before you ask him (Matt 6:6–8).

In other words, when you pray, enter into a private dialogue where God may reward you in secret. Note that when you are speaking with another person, the atmosphere is different than when you are alone. And prayer is not meant to be a monologue but a dialogue. When you pray, do so with the faith-generated atmosphere that God is truly listening, and will respond to you in God's timing and way. In other words, *a prayer state is a form of mutual atmosphere*, just like having an honest and heartfelt dialogue with a loved one, someone who knows you right well, so that you can speak "shorthand" rather than "longhand."

Once in a prayer state, you can learn to stay there for longer periods. And even though you will have thoughts, feelings, and the like distract you, not *all of you will be distracted*. You can continue to be anchored to a prayer state in the midst of whatever distracts you. Once distracted, while still

29

connected to your prayer state, you can gently return your full attention to God, never having completely abandoned your prayer state.

Prayer states can be of varying lengths and intensities. At the highest level of prayer intensity, you can enter into what is termed "ecstasy" or an "ecstatic state of being." The word *ecstasy* comes from the Greek language and means literally "to stand outside oneself." It can be a delightful rapture, a temporary but extreme happiness. In the context of a prayer state, ecstasy means to stand outside your embodied single self in the world, while standing in the Spirit of God. It is nothing to fear; rather, it is a wondrous moment of pure mutuality with God. And as such, it is to be sought, accepted, and freely entered every time it is available to you in prayer. Entering it is the first thing I do every single morning, as I turn fully to the Beloved.

Just after a precious prayer state, I wrote to God:

Tenderly, how tenderly have you come upon me in our brief seasons of silent communion, you in me, and I in you. You have touched my soul more surely, more serenely than fingers can caress flesh.

I have experienced you experiencing me as none other, knowing just where and when and how I needed to be touched, wanted to be touched, even if I did not know it until you touched me.

The way you seemed to succor and savor me—what can I say to you, do for you in response, other than say how I love you, how I praise you for your way with me?

Would that I could touch you as you have touched me. Would that I could caress your Spirit as you have caressed my soul.

Does my desire to touch you, touch you? Does my will to caress you, caress you?

When I shed this shroud of flesh, I will learn what our relationship has come to, and whether my straining in my restraints to touch you, touched you.

PRAYER AND LOVE

IN TERMS OF INTENSITY and longevity, the greatest human need is to give oneself to love, while in love. As the poet Tagore said, "I am only waiting for love, to give myself up at last into his hands." Only through so doing may you attain the most valuable prize possible in this life: union with love. And since God is love, that means to give yourself to God, while in God.

This can only happen through prayer, while in prayer. That means: prayer permits the most profound and total self-giving and self-receiving of all possible human activities. As language first began and ever ends in God, so too love itself begins in God and shall return to God, having lost nothing of itself. Rather, love, through all of its moments, its joys and its sorrows, its triumphs and its defeats alike, only and always gains more of itself through human participation. Adding love to love just may be the ultimate reason and purpose of human life.

I have envisioned my final self-giving to the God who is Love in these words:

The time for gathering is approaching. What I may take and what I must leave I will know only when the unseen door between us opens and you restore my sight.

The gathering is drawing nearer. I pray you will give me sufficient time to gather my life before you gather my soul. What I may remember and what I must forget I will learn only when I pass through your portal of no return.

The gathering is not the harvesting, but the taking up and embracing of all that has been, with a thankfulness words cannot express, though tears may release.

At the gathering you will permit me that last look, as if gazing back to behold for the first and only time before it disappears behind the mist of what is no more, the full mountain range of the life I have lived. I will hold this sweeping vision of my life tightly to my heart, all I have received and given and shared and known, all my joys and sorrows, all my loves and lessons learned. I will see, without buffers or barriers, the truth my life came to.

At that solemn height I will, as much as I ever shall, know myself as you have known me, known me even before I began the journey across the expansive range of my rearing.

And just before I turn away, just before I cross over into you, I will offer you a grateful sighing of my whole being.

And with my thankfulness laid before you like a wedding runner, I will give myself to you at last.

Your daily prayers are, in hidden fact, preparation for this holy moment of final self-giving, which for God will also signify your self-receiving. Thus are prayer and love inseparable. Only through prayer may you enter into the Trinity of love, who is God: the endless circle of the lover, the beloved, and the love itself. The eternal renewing energy of divine love is revealed in its endless total self-giving, self-receiving, and self-sharing. Truly, love holds nothing back from itself.

Let this love be your prayer platform and motif.

PRAYER AND SPACE

ONE OF THE GREAT prayer questions is where exactly prayer happens. Medieval theologian Meister Eckhart said that you can only experience God in God's own space. Does God occupy "space"? Yes, but you cannot see God's space, which is also God's kingdom. Nor can you see 95 percent of the space of the physical universe, which physics and astronomy say is *not* empty. Space is one of the great mysteries, as is time and the connection between the two.

The truth is, your "I" or soul cannot be seen by anyone except God. You cannot even see yourself, but only your embodied being together with the self-images you generate, along with the helpful and harmful input of others. Though the "space" of your inner being may be real to you, it is nevertheless still immeasurable, be it tiny or immense. Likewise, the invisible "space" between you and others, which is really a kind of shared or mutual space, sensed especially in love relationships, is actually as real as internal and external space. The space where prayer happens and unfolds is at once both within you and between you and God.

This means that regardless of your outer circumstances, even if you should be physically housed in a small prison cell, you can still enter into the vastness of the space between you and God. Call it the "universe of persons," which exists invisibly together with the "universe of matter," 95 percent of which is also invisible. These two constitute infinite sections or dimensions of the "multiverse" of theoretical physics.

Prayer happens both within and between you and God. You enter into the yet to be fully realized universe of persons, where you began before your birth, and where we will end up after your time of embodied being here is over. This means that through prayer, *you are never trapped in the physical universe.* It is not as if you can fully enter into heaven, which you cannot as long as you remain in the flesh; but you can get into immediate communion with the God who is vast beyond measure or comprehension. These words are trustworthy and true.

Jesus says that "you will know the truth, and the truth will make you free" (John 8:32). The reality is this: prayer constitutes your true and everlasting freedom. What happens in prayer is strictly between you and God. No person or power can prevent your prayer togetherness with God. As Paul insists: "For freedom Christ has set us free. Stand firm, therefore, and do not submit again to a yoke of slavery" (Gal 5:1).

Jesus also indicates that the kingdom of God is "in your midst" (Luke 17:21). That same verse is just as correctly translated as "within you." The Greek preposition used in this verse is *entos*, and it means both "within" and "between" or among. Thus, prayer happens simultaneously within you and between you and God. How this is so really cannot be explained or even grasped, but only moved into, in faith and freedom. That is where prayer happens, and where your true freedom awaits your entrance in the shared space with God, which is your destined eternal home.

PRAYER AND TIME

THERE IS CLOCK TIME, then there is relational time. They are not the same thing. Clock time is horizontal and measurable; relational time is between persons when they connect. It has simple duration, is vertical, and is immeasurable. Relational time may be temporary compared to the constancy of clock time, but its aftereffects can be permanent.

Prayer unfolds in relational time. Like a conversation with a beloved friend, prayer time may seem brief yet clock time could indicate that hours went by. The opposite can seem just as true: prayer time may seem long, while the concurrent clock time was surprisingly brief. Speaking for myself, I have brief prayer moments throughout the day, turning intensely to the ultimate Love of my eternal life. Such brief "God-fullness moments" are of a peace-bearing depth. And they render clock time irrelevant.

Both clock and relational time are precious. Yet so many of us do not engage in sufficient relational time, not only for prayer, but also for love. And perhaps we wonder what God might want of us. Is God demanding more time than we are willing or able to give? If so, a mixture of fear and guilt might arise within us.

When guilt enters a love relationship, one of two outcomes typically occurs. We either confess and apologize, or we avoid the other and let the relationship slowly slide into our history. Take for example grown children who have moved away from home and have not kept up connecting with their parents. Guilt will likely show up. It sure did between me and my mother. It seemed I was always apologizing, with an "I am sorry I have not called you."

Since God is our Eternal Parent, we might have similar feelings: apologize and/or avoid. Yet the gracious truth is that God simply wants to hear our voice, as do Mom and Dad. Rather than wanting to make us feel guilty, God wants to embrace us with love, as did the father of the prodigal son upon the latter's return, in Jesus' parable about how God loves us (Luke 15:20–24). God will not lay guilt on us; that is something we lay on ourselves. God will not reject us, but like Mom or Dad, really wants to hear from us, to get a sense as to where we are, to keep our relationship active. And when you turn to God with your whole being, you are granted an immediate audience, whether or not you sense it.

Time will remain an issue all of our lives. And that includes time for prayer. How much time is needed? How much time do you have? How little? Do you feel guilty or sad or stressed about praying? *Prayer should never be a negative issue*. Quite the opposite. It should be a time away from all stress and guilt, a time to let go of everything and to let God be God.

Jesus tells us we can keep our words few and time in prayer brief (Matt 6:5–8). Even single-word prayers like "Help!" or "Thanks!" can be sufficient, for God knows what we are really saying and meaning better than we do.

What usually does take some time is attaining a "prayer state," which is a heightened time with God, without needing words, but having a serene sense of pure connection with the Beloved. Then time *for* becomes time *with*. And there is no greater time than being together with God, even if it be for a brief yet immeasurable period.

PRAYER AND HURRY

HAVE YOU EVER TRIED to hurry taking a breath, say before diving underwater? Your body almost resists you. In ordinary circumstances, your lungs operate automatically, without you needing to attend to whether or not to breathe, or how much to take in and for how long. You are born breathing and you can never stop as long as you are in the flesh.

You are also born to pray. Your soul needs regular intakes of the Spirit, as your lungs need air. Interesting that both Spirit and air share the same word in the Greek New Testament: *pneuma*. And just like your lungs in breathing, your soul does not want to be rushed in prayer. Do not hurry prayer, even if you are in a hurry. You cannot speed up the entrance into a prayer state. A "rush to relax" is as much an oxymoron as "speed up to slow down." Remember that God knows your thoughts and heart before you pray; God knows what you want to say before you do. It is you who may need to put into words what you do not yet know is bubbling up within you.

Rather than attempting to rush a prayer, just say and mean and feel the power of a single word, like "Help!" That is really all you need to say, especially when it is heartfelt. God will know what stands behind your plea. Then trust that God has heard your single-word prayer. The "heartfelt" is more important to God than the words. Jesus said, "When you are praying, do not heap up empty phrases as the Gentiles do; for they think that they will be heard because of their many words. Do not be like them, for your Father knows what you need before you ask him" (Matt 6:7–8).

Yet much in our lives seems to demand that we hurry, whether it is the insistence of an impatient child to "do for me now!," or the demands of a stressed out boss to "finish this project today!" Psychologist Carl Jung said, "Hurry is not only of the devil; hurry is the devil." When you are in a hurry, it becomes difficult to determine what matters more and what matters less. Values tend to flatten out as pressure and stress build. In a harried hurry we wonder, "What must I do? What can I do? And in what order should I do these things, including praying?" And where there is hurry, guilt is not far behind, as is defensiveness. When we are unable to do what we want to do, or believe that we are supposed to do, in the space of time it may take us, our frustration can easily prompt us to seek to justify ourselves before God.

God already loves you, and sent Jesus Christ to show you how much. One thing about Jesus in the Gospels: He never seemed to be in a hurry. Rather, wherever Jesus went, he was fully present to whomever He met there. So in prayer, just show up; be fully present there, where God already is. Focus more on the pleasing content of your prayer, rather than its length.

PRAYER AND LAUGHTER

YOU MAY NOT LAUGH as you pray, or pray while you laugh, but prayer and humor have some crucial elements in common. Both help to lift you out of a situation, or the feeling of being trapped by the circumstances of your life. That is, they offer you an immediate way of stepping back from, if not transcending, your current conditions. Prayer and laughter free your inner being, even if it is only for a time.

Some of the best laughter I have been fortunate to share has been with families at hospitals while awaiting the results of surgery, or worse, an expected approaching end of life for a loved one. It is not of course as if the circumstances were anything less than grave, or that they were laughing at its seriousness. Rather, the humor, just like prayer, gave them temporary relief, a brief lifting of burdens, a short forgetfulness, helping to rebalance their listing souls.

In philosopher Friedrich Nietzsche's view, the religiously stiff and hypocritical persons were those who claimed that there were things about which one must never laugh. I have known such humorless persons, and I felt sorry for them, even if my own sense of humor was upsetting to them and their sad misunderstanding of the Christian faith.

I had a very real dream, if not a visitation, during seminary in which an angel was sitting above me on our bedpost, legs crossed and looking down at me. The angel said one thing, which woke me up immediately. Even though it was many years ago, that statement from heaven remains vivid. Though I could not see the angel's face, the words were spoken with apparent understanding and warmth. The angel said, "Yes, Hal, God does have a sense of humor."

One of the greatest laughs in biblical history came out of Abraham's wife Sarah, when, at age ninety, God said she would finally, after twenty-five years of waiting, give birth to a son. Though she denied laughing to God, God told her to name the child "Isaac," which means "he laughs," or simply "laughter." Rather than criticizing Sarah for her laughter, God wanted her laugh remembered and celebrated. Nothing is impossible for God.

The one who laughs last, laughs best. In your destined tomorrow, the best laughter will yet be yours. Jesus said: "Blessed are you who weep now, for you will laugh" (Luke 6:21b).

PRAYER AND "THE ONE"

IF YOU SEEK GOD, you are already sought by God. For God is not cruel and will not put such a desire in you without intending to eventually fulfill it. When, where, and how God will do so, you cannot know until it actually unfolds. Your task is to persevere sufficiently to demonstrate to God—and also to yourself—how much you seek God. And you must seek God for *God*, not for any other benefits, which could render your search unacceptable.

Why do we seek a human life partner? So that "special other" can gratify our needs and desires? In order to make us feel better about ourselves and our lot? So that we no longer have to face the future alone? Or is it because we want to love and be loved by the "right" person? Perhaps all of the above, in varying degrees.

Romantic love is a mystery not reducible to physical attraction. Rather, there is always this "something more" or "something else" in addition to biology and even psychology. I say this on the basis not only of my own marriage of more than fifty years, but also by having performed more than three hundred weddings, including a thousand hours of premarriage counseling. In addition, I established and directed a matchmaking service that developed with more than six hundred clients. Add to that hundreds of hours conducting marriage counseling. *Romantic love is a primal mystery*, at least the falling in love part. Such mysterious love is actually a "*spiritual organism*" between two persons, and them alone. Once in love, they must learn how to stay in love, since love alone is not enough for the long term. And both must work together.

Do you believe, or at least hope, that there is "the one" out there whom you have already found or for whom you continue to search, in order to love and be loved by, and to live together in love? Have you been looking only for that special human other? How about God as your "Ultimate Other"? The search for God as your "Other" is the ultimate search, because when you do find God, at the same time God finds you, and you will at last grasp the true and final meaning of "the One." God is destined to be your ultimate and

41

eternal Spouse, from whom you come and for whom you were created, to abide together in a union without end.

When you finally encounter God in prayer, you will know and know that you know of a certainty, that God has always been and will always be, the one and only "One." I simply cannot overstate this: you were made by God, for God. And apart from God, try though you may, there will remain this inexplicable and immeasurable "hole" in your being, which God alone can fill.

PRAYER AS VERTICAL AND HORIZONTAL

PRAYER HAS BOTH A vertical and horizontal dimension. And to have a full and complete prayer life, you must engage in both. The vertical is the "I-Thou" relationship between God and you alone, one-to-one, rather like a marriage relationship. This form of prayer has been termed "the flight of the alone to the Alone." Jesus was referring to this profoundly personal vertical prayer when he said, "But whenever you pray, go into your room and shut the door and pray to your Father who is in secret; and your Father who sees in secret will reward you" (Matt 6:6). There are no words to satisfactorily describe this "secret" relationship between you as lover and God as your Beloved. In the divine-human reciprocity, God will likewise call you "beloved."

Horizontal prayer is when you join together to pray with others. Jesus was referring to this extremely important and necessary connection of mutual life with God when he said, "For where two or three are gathered in my name, I am there among them" (Matt 18:20). This constitutes the heart of the church as the "body of Christ." In my years as a parish pastor, communal prayer was a constant activity, from weekly worship services to small groups and healing prayer teams. I call this "horizontal" prayer because it spreads out to include more than one person addressing God. And it is a vital opportunity for us to share our vertical relationship with God with each other, expanding our singular "I-Thou" to include their own "I-Thou" relationship with God. By this means the "we" of the body of Christ comes into evidence.

I first encountered the Holy Spirit as a part of a newly convened college prayer group. The horizontal community prayer opened up the door to the vertical connection to God. Over the years, I learned the unseen yet present truth of Jesus' words: when we join in his name, Christ is in spiritual fact there, among and between us. This is something that simply cannot happen in private prayer. It is as if Christ wants us to pray together, and will on occasion reward us with signs of his presence and healing power.

At the same time, I require daily prayer time alone with the Beloved, so my "just-between-us" relationship can continue to flourish. The incomprehensible miracle is that just as I have my own marital-like relationship with God, so also do countless others. Somehow, God manages to combine the exclusive with the inclusive. And who but God can do that?

THE FIELD OF PRAYER

PRAYER CAN BE THE conduit for an entrance into a kind of spiritual gravitation field. And in its most intense unitive moments, prayer may be compared to an electromagnetic field. At some point, not likely during this life, though possibly, you may enter permanently into what could accurately be termed the "Spirit Field" of God. I entered into God's invisible tractor beam in August 2003. It was during a ten-day intensive centering prayer retreat, when through a chain of events, my heart passed into an unending union with the Sacred Heart of Jesus Christ.

Fortunately for my sanity, I am not the first person to have had such a heart-to-Heart bonding with Christ. I wrote a book about it and its possible significance for humanity in 2018: *The Heart of Jesus and the Coming Relationship*.

To extend the magnetic field analogy, imagine that you heart is actually a kind of magnet. You do not know this, of course, until the Heart of Christ draws near. Here is how Bernard of Clairvaux (1090–1153) described it nearly a thousand years ago:

> You ask then how I knew he was present, when his ways can in no way be traced? He is life and power, and as soon as he enters in, he awakens my slumbering soul; he stirs and soothes and pierces my heart . . . It was not by any movement of his that I recognized his coming; it was not by any of my senses that I perceived he had penetrated to the depths of my being. Only by the movement of my heart . . . did I perceive his presence; and I knew the power of his might because my faults were put to flight and my human yearnings brought into subjection.

When Christ draws near, your heart will stir like a magnet awakening to its other, generating an invisible but ever so real field, between the two poles of the relationship. This forms a kind of trinity: the two poles and the magnetic field between them, which joins and keeps them together. The generation of this heart-to-Heart Field between you and Jesus Christ can happen during what I call "abiding prayer," which I will present to you later.

I think that Paul was likely describing this Spirit Field when he wrote: "For I am convinced that neither death, nor life, nor angels, nor rulers, nor things present, nor things to come, nor powers, nor height, nor depth, nor anything else in all creation, will be able to separate us from the love of God in Christ Jesus our Lord" (Rom 8:38–39).

PRAYER AND THE TRINITY

IT IS IMPORTANT TO give you something of a technical vision of prayer in relation to the Holy Trinity. To begin with, theology, or "God-talk," is really a game of prepositions. As regards Christian prayer, that signifies that prayer unfolds *in* the Person of the Son, *to* the Person of the Father, and *through* the Person of the Holy Spirit. In relational terms, this means when you pray, you secretly enter into Christ, who is your "Eternal I," while addressing God the Father, who is your "Eternal You," through the Holy Spirit, who is your "Eternal We" shared with God.

That means *prayer is essentially relational*; it happens between you and God, while unfolding in and through God. That also means prayer is less what you do and more what you enter into, namely the eternal We of the Spirit between the eternal I and the eternal You of God.

Most significantly, this also means that the divine *relationship* is as ultimate and eternal, as the divine *persons* who share in it. The "Three-in-One" Trinity represents the eternal structure of persons, not only divine but also human, since we are made in God's image (Gen 1:27). The divine-human relationship, which Christ has opened up and made available to us, constitutes our very salvation, our endless and unbreakable "We" with God (see Rom 8:35–39).

All this may sound profound and complicated, and it is. Yet at the same time it is as simple and understandable as any conversation with another person with whom you have shared, and hopefully still share. Think of your relationship with your mother, and/or your father. Think of your most significant friendships. And most importantly, think of romantic love, of falling in love, of marriage and all it entails. As the Bible puts it: the two shall "become one flesh" (Gen 2:24). So also shall you become one in soul and spirit with Christ. Paul says that "anyone united to the Lord becomes one spirit with him" (1 Cor 6:17).

Relationships are where we "live and move and have our being," as Paul put it in his sermon in front of the Areopagus in Athens (Acts 17:28).

That includes your being together as well as your being alone. With God and in God abides your true and eternal being, your "I," which you will share forever with Christ. As Jesus said, "I am the way, and the truth, and the life. No one comes to the Father except through me" (John 14:6).

As you continue to pray, you will eventually realize that prayer never really ends, nor will your love relationship with God.

THE ULTIMATE
GOAL OF PRAYER

THERE ARE DIFFERENT REASONS to pray, and different things to pray for. And God hears and honors prayer of all kinds. Yet *the ultimate goal of prayer is union with God.* Now for most of us, of course, that is a long way off. And that is just fine; God is not in a hurry, and neither should we be. It is like taking a long journey across the United States, from Maine to California. Or slowly, meditatively walking along a labyrinth, where the going is almost as important as the arriving. As long as you keep on the path set before you by God and those who have walked it before you, you will eventually get there, wherever the "there" is you seek. Yet it is helpful to have a sense of where you are headed before you start down the spiritual path. If you have no idea exactly what your destination is, you could get easily sidetracked and not even know it.

Over time you will begin your prayer by permitting yourself to be just where you are, even if you are not sure where that is. If you are lost in the woods, stay where you happen to be, and let others find you. Just so, God will always find you where you are and gently take you to where God wants you to be, if you are willing to be led by God. And where is that? Call it "mutual indwelling." That means simply being together, in the secret space God establishes for you two to abide together.

This mutual indwelling is what Jesus is praying we will attain through God's grace in his great "priestly prayer," offered for our sake in an unending plea: "As you, Father, are in me and I am in you, may they also be in us, so that the world may believe that you have sent me. The glory that you have given me I have given them, so that they may be one, as we are one, I in them and you in me, that they may become completely one, so that the world may know that you have sent me and have loved them even as you have loved me" (John 17:21–23).

Back in February of 2009, while I was engaged in a time of silent prayer, I sensed the subtle approach of Jesus Christ, over against me. I could not make him out, of course; it was as if Christ's silhouette appeared before me. I could not glimpse Christ's face or the content of his spiritual form, but only his silhouette, only his barest outline. Christ came calmly, seeming to sit directly across from me, perhaps not wanting to disturb or distress me.

I didn't know what else to do but keep on praying, waiting to see what would happen next. After a time of silently sensing Christ facing me, he seemed to throw a large mantle over the top of me, the sign and seal of his prophetic ministry. It reminded me immediately of the exchange between the prophet Elijah and his disciple, Elisha. Having been commanded by God to anoint Elisha as a prophet in his place, Elijah threw his mantle over Elisha (1 Kgs 19:19). In ancient days, a mantle was one's all-purpose outerwear, designed to protect one from wind, rain, and cold. At once, and perhaps foolishly, I desired whatever of Christ's prophetic ministry he was willing to share with me. There we were, strangely together underneath this temporary tent of his prophetic presence.

No words were spoken. We were simply face-to-face for a time—not readily measurable during the prayer itself. It could have been thirty minutes or thirty seconds. The impact would have been just as vivid and lasting. Finally, I asked Jesus a single question, telepathically. I was surprised at my question, one which seemed to arise spontaneously, without forethought. I asked, "What is your mission?"

To my surprise, his words came in rapid response. It was as if Christ wanted me to ask this question, wanted to be forthcoming with the information, which may have been why he showed up, to share these words, which would have a permanent impact on my understanding of God, and my life's work for God.

Jesus said, in a "voiceless echo": "To bring humanity into union with God."

Abiding with Christ, under his mantle of mission, it hit me that his mission was now mine as well, that I would serve as yet another witness or emissary of his great work. Nothing less than union will satisfy God or fully satisfy the human heart. Once the significance of Christ's words hit me, the mantle and silhouette disappeared. Point made, presence vanished.

FINAL PREPARATION FOR PRAYER: HOW TO APPROACH GOD

YOUR IMAGE OR UNDERSTANDING of God largely determines how you will approach God. And how you approach God, along with your expectations going in, significantly affect what happens or does not happen during and after an attempted prayer connection.

The question is: how best to approach God? The answer is as simple as it is profound. *When you approach God, do so as if you are approaching love itself.* For in hidden fact, that is precisely what you are doing. And listen for God as you would listen for the voice of love. Now the only way to approach God is through prayer, however you understand prayer. Even to question whether God exists, let alone whether God knows and loves you, cannot be asked of God without entering into prayer. Prayer is communication with God in all its forms. Crying out to an "unknown God" in anger or fear is actually a powerful prayer, which will be answered in God's timing and way. And God's apparent silence can teach us patience, perseverance, and faith, the faith that must become as unconditional as God's love for us is already unconditional.

The apostle John, who well understood love, equates God with love, and love with God:

> Beloved, let us love one another, because love is from God; everyone who loves is born of God and knows God. Whoever does not love does not know God, for God is love . . . So we have known and believe the love that God has for us. God is love, and those who abide in love abide in God, and God abides in them.
>
> Love has been perfected among us in this: that we may have boldness on the day of judgment, because as he is, so are we in this world. There is no fear in love, but perfect love casts out

51

fear; for fear has to do with punishment, and whoever fears has not reached perfection in love. We love because he first loved us (1 John 4:7–8, 16–19).

Please note that the Greek word translated as "perfect" in this passage is *teleia*, which really means mature, fully grown, like an ear of corn. It has finally become what it is supposed to be; hence, it is perfect. Perfect does not mean sinless or flawless.

The most succinct and profound description of God's love is found in Paul's first letter to the church at Corinth. The unique Greek word used here for love, and also in the passage above is *agape*. *Agape* love is overflowingly full, and seeks to give to all who are desirous of receiving, all who thirst for and will gladly drink in love. As you read and meditate on these holy words, exchange the word "love" for "God," and see how the passage affects your heart: "Love is patient; love is kind; love is not envious or boastful or arrogant or rude. It does not insist on its own way; it is not irritable or resentful; it does not rejoice in wrongdoing, but rejoices in the truth. It bears all things, believes all things, hopes all things, endures all things. Love never ends" (1 Cor 13:4–8).

It is important to note that the Greek verb (*pipteo*) translated as "ends" in the NRSV, is translated as "fails" in the New International and New King James versions. This Greek word carries both meanings, as does love. That means neither love nor God ultimately *ever ends or fails*.

The central question now arises: how are you to approach God as love itself? To do so certainly excludes a fear-laden image of God as judging, angry, vengeful, and jealous. Would you then approach the Love-God with awe, desire, hope, excitement, and faith, or with fear, pessimism, and doubt? How could this Love-God ever be impersonal? I invite you to meditate on this question, as you pray through the two Scripture passages quoted above.

What would your life be like if you truly believed and acted out of the conviction that God is love, and love is God, so that whatever is not of love, is not of God. And just as importantly, whatever is of love is also of God.

In personal response, I offer my own answer to what my life would be like if God were love itself:

If you are love, then I am yours, completely, wholly, with all that I am, and with all that I can be, now and forever.

If you are love, then it is all too simple, beyond word descriptions, just so simple that it belies measure, like the sea below and the stars above.

If you are love, then theories and theologies falter and fail, like humorless anecdotes upon silent heights, vain attempts of pride to produce truth which stands unseen, unmade, and unknown before it.

If you are love, then the world makes sense, meaning matters, yet mystery abides, touching but untouchable, and I already know what I need to know; and am able to do what I must do, through the love you are and give.

And that, I am blessed to say, is how I approach God.

BREATH PRAYERS

"Close your eyes. Breathe in and out slowly. You are changing your vibration by just slowing down."

—Archangel Sandalphon

"Prayer is the breath of your life which gives you the freedom to go and stay where you wish and to find the many signs which point out the way to a new land."

—Henri J. M. Nouwen

"Prayer is the breath of life to our soul; holiness is impossible without it."

—Mother Teresa

ABOUT BREATH PRAYERS

BREATH PRAYERS ARE PERHAPS the easiest way to begin to develop your prayer life. They can be brief, like five or ten minutes, and can be slowly lengthened as you become more disciplined and habitual in praying.

Most significantly, the word for "breath" in the original Greek of the New Testament is *pneuma*, which is also the word for "air" as well as "spirit." This mode of prayer focuses on your breathing, specifically on your breathing in and breathing out. Attending to your breath makes it easier to remain focused. This prayer is as simple as breathing in and out, something you do constantly.

It would be helpful to practice "*belly breathing*." It is also called "diaphragmatic breathing," which has a number of health benefits, from lowering stress to controlling blood pressure. It involves expanding your belly out as you breathe in. Here is the process for breath prayers:

1. Sit in a comfortable chair, with back support. Have both your feet on the ground. Put your hands on your thighs, and close your eyes.

2. Relax your shoulders.

3. Breathe in through your nose, while expanding your belly outwards.

4. Hold your breath for a second or two.

5. Breathe out as gently and slowly as your breathed in. You can breathe out through your nose or your mouth, whichever feels more comfortable.

6. Continue this way of breathing in and out through the entire prayer. After a time, the breathing rhythm will become automatic, and your relaxation almost immediate.

One of the advantages of breath prayers is that they take your attention off the number one problem of prayer, namely distractions, brought about by thinking. Here is the problem: your mind never stops thinking. Even during all five of the stages of sleep, if someone woke you up, you could always report what you were thinking at that moment. So in prayer, you need to learn to let go of rather than wrestle with your thoughts. Whatever you wrestle with, you cannot get free from—as long as you wrestle.

Like the flowing of a river, let your thoughts go where they go, ceasing to attend to them. This is of course difficult; but with practice and God's help, it is doable. In so doing, there will be moments of forgetfulness of the river, which then seems to stop temporarily. These moments are gifts of grace. They bring you into the mysterious time of connection and communion with God. Call it the "time between the seconds."

In what follows, I will offer ten different breath prayers. See which ones work best for you now, in drawing you closer to connecting with God.

PRAYER FOR PEACE

To ATTAIN PEACE, NOT only must you seek it, but you must also be willing to receive it. Like faith, peace is something you have to choose every day, sometimes every hour. What does peace really mean? *Peace means harmonious connection with something or someone.* Indeed, the root of the word "peace" means "to fasten," or "to confirm an agreement." Thus, connection is at the heart of peace; peace always includes a *"with"* of association—or there is no peace. That is, peace has to do with the state that can exist between two or more beings, including your relationship with yourself, for you do have a unique kind of relationship with yourself.

Peace is the harmony of interconnected well-being, with three primary dimensions. First, peace signifies the absence of dis-ease, infirmity, and discord, whether of body, soul, spirit, or relationship. Second, peace is a positive, harmonious connection with oneself, including body, soul, and spirit. Third, peace is a right relationship with God, and built on that, a right relationship with each other, which is God's will for us.

Let us begin with a breath prayer for peace, lasting five to ten minutes, which you can lengthen as the Spirit guides you. Seated comfortably in a straight-back chair, breathe in the peace of Christ, which Jesus gave us and is beyond our understanding. Then yield to that peace as you breathe out. Imagine the peace of Christ being all around you, ever available to you just like air, if and as you are ready to breathe it in, and exhale all resistance.

Breathe in peace, and as you breathe out, yield to that peace. Continue breathing in peace and breathing out yielding yourself to that peace.

Take to heart Jesus' words: "Peace I leave with you; my peace I give to you. I do not give to you as the world gives. Do not let your hearts be troubled, and do not let them be afraid" (John 14:27). In Christ, there is peace, always peace. Jesus said: "I have said this to you, so that in me you may have peace" (John 16:33). Christ's peace, which is beyond our understanding, is the faith conviction that all will be well eternally. If you believe that everything will end well, you can more readily face and endure what you must on the way to eternal well-being.

Paul experienced the peace of Christ who forgave him his past life and motivated his mission to humanity. Paul said: "Now may the Lord of peace himself give you peace at all times in all ways" (2 Thess 3:16).

As you silently breathe in peace, you will come to feel more at peace. Then in brief periods during your day, again breathe in peace and breathe out yielding to that peace. Let it become a comforting rhythm.

PRAYER FOR LOVE

LOVE IS THE GREATEST of all the gifts of the Spirit of God. In truth, love is more than a gift; it *is* God, for "God is love" (1 John 4:8, 16). God's love for us makes possible our love for God in response, as well as our love for humanity. The words of the apostle John make this very clear:

> Beloved, let us love one another; for love is of God, and he who loves is born of God and knows God. He who does not love does not know God; for God is love . . . So we know and believe the love God has for us. God is love, and he who abides in love abides in God, and God abides in him. In this is love perfected with us, that we may have confidence for the day of judgment, because as he is, so are we in this world. There is no fear in love, but perfect love casts out fear. For fear has to do with punishment, and he who fears is not perfected in love. We love, because he first loved us. (1 John 4:7–8, 17–19)

In this simple breath prayer, sitting comfortably in a straight-back chair and "belly breathing," breathe in God's love, which is with and around you constantly, awaiting your discovery. And when you breathe out, breathe out love for God, in response to God's love for you. *Breathe in love and breathe out more love.* Let in the greatest of all God's gifts, God's very own love, love for you and love through you to others. Love can only be freely received as a sheer gift, ever undeserved and unwarranted—yet there for you, nonetheless. There is no greater or more necessary "leap of faith" than to receive, even to overflowing, this gift of God's love. It is only God's love that can fully empower your love for God, love for others, and also love for yourself, freely given in response to God's free gift of love.

Pray this Scripture before and after the breathing exercise, as a way to gain greater love: "As the Father has loved me, so I have loved you; abide in my love. If you keep my commandments, you will abide in my love, just as I have kept my Father's commandments and abide in his love . . . This is my commandment, that you love one another as I have loved you (John 15:9–10, 12).

PRAYER FOR FAITH

FAITH IS ONE OF the most significant and needed gifts of God. Therefore, you can seek more faith, as did the father who asked Jesus, right before Jesus healed his son, "I believe; help my unbelief!" (Mark 9:24). You can always ask Christ to increase your faith, as did the apostles: "The apostles said to the Lord, 'Increase our faith!' The Lord replied, 'If you had faith the size of a mustard seed, you could say to this mulberry tree, 'Be uprooted and planted in the sea,' and it would obey you'" (Luke 17:5–6).

The writer of the letter to the Hebrews said, simply: "Now faith is the assurance of things hoped for, the conviction of things not seen" (Heb 11:1). And as I have written:

Faith is a God-made bridge from your heart to heaven, a span immovable, indestructible.

Take the risk and venture out; not looking down but straight ahead toward God's clouded presence.

Let your yearning heart energize you to walk to the One who awaits you, without fear of falling or failure.

Faith is a hidden knowledge of what is to come, a heavenly manna to daily feed your heart.

Believe in, trust that veiled knowledge.

Faith is the inexplicable conviction that regardless of short-term outcomes, all will be well, eternally.

Faith will never fail you; if you but listen to it,

It will make you right with God; in truth, faith is a place of right standing with God.

And when you are right with God, fear is reduced to a nuisance, calling at you from below, but never able to touch God's hallowed bridge.

I invite you to engage in a breath prayer for faith. Sitting comfortably in a straight-back chair, with both feet on the ground, engage in "belly breathing." With each breath, breathe in God's gift of faith, which always surrounds you as the atmosphere of heaven; and in yielding response, breathe out trust. Continue breathing in ever greater faith and exhaling ever greater trust. Let your growing faith convict your heart that all will indeed be well, eternally.

PRAYER FOR HOPE

THE THING ABOUT HOPE is that it always wants to have the final word. We cannot live long or well without hope. Hope lingers on between our breathing in and breathing out. While there is breath in the body, there is always some residue of hope in the soul. And with it being one of the great gifts of the Holy Spirit, we can and even must ask for more.

And where are you to place your hopes? The psalmist says, "Hope in the LORD from this time on and forevermore" (Ps 131:3). And the writer of the letter to the Hebrews says, "We have this hope, a sure and steadfast anchor of the soul, a hope that enters the inner shrine behind the curtain" (Heb 6:19).

I remember several years ago receiving an unexpected rejection letter from a publisher. Hope seemed to drain from my soul, as I walked back from a hike to a monastery where I was conducting a men's prayer retreat. Suddenly, without warning, a puff of the breath of the Spirit brushed against my chest, instantly uplifting my soul. In a flash, it renewed my hope in God and in God's wisdom and will.

What I realized afresh was this: *place your hopes in God alone*, rather than in this or that possible outcome. The greater your expectations of some favorable outcome, the greater will be your disappointment should it not come about. Though nothing is impossible for God, God looks to our eternal well-being, rather than only our temporary, here-and-now-only happiness.

The bottom line for me is this: I do not know how God will do it, but I have secured my hope anchor-like in God and I wait for God's will for me to unfold fully—which will likely not happen in this life. Psalm 130:5–7 speaks the substance of my hope: "I wait for the LORD, my soul waits, and in his word I hope" (Ps 130:5).

And with the apostle Paul, here is my prayer for you: "May the God of hope fill you with all joy and peace in believing, so that you may abound in hope by the power of the Holy Spirit" (Rom 15:13).

Now let us pray a breath prayer for hope. "Belly breathing," breathe in hope, which always surrounds you, as does the Spirit. When you exhale, breathe out assurance of future well-being, as your soul quietly receives more and more up building from the Spirit, as you continue breathing in God's priceless gift of hope. It is rather like your soul becoming re-oxygenated.

PRAYER FOR JOY

JOY ARRIVES AT THE same time you actually get something you have been seeking. It could be finally seeing and embracing a beloved friend or family member, after a time of missing them. It could be receiving some longed-for good news, say of good health or financial success. Such human joy is relatively short-lived. Like a wave hitting a beach, it tends to pull back at about the same speed it first reached the shore of your soul. Even if you want your joy to stay longer, it does not usually agree. Like adapting to a pleasant smell, you get accustomed to it too quickly.

The joy of the Lord, however, is a different kind of joy. As one of the fruits of the Holy Spirit, this joy arrives immediately when you experience *God in you and yourself in God*. And it resists pulling away. And you can re-enter it while in prayer, as a vivid memory that continues to reactivate itself, as you realize afresh that God is in you, and you are in God.

Jesus told his disciples, shortly before he would die for us: "In a little while the world will no longer see me, but you will see me; because I live, you also will live. On that day you will know that I am in my Father, and you in me, and I in you" (John 14:19–20).

Jesus continued:

> I have said these things to you so that my joy may be in you, and that your joy may be complete . . . Very truly, I tell you, you will weep and mourn, but the world will rejoice; you will have pain, but your pain will turn into joy. When a woman is in labor, she has pain, because her hour has come. But when her child is born, she no longer remembers the anguish because of the joy of having brought a human being into the world. So you have pain now; but I will see you again, and your hearts will rejoice, and no one will take your joy from you. (John 15:11; 16:20–22)

"No one will take your joy from you." What an extraordinary promise. You will have a joy that cannot be taken away from you, regardless of your

circumstances. Imagine a circumstance-free joy. This is possible only as a sheer gift of God.

So here is a breath prayer: breathe in "God is in me," and breathe out, "and I am in God." Then let the joy of the Spirit fill you with the truth, the power, and the eternity of these words.

PRAYER FOR GRATITUDE

GIVING THANKS BRINGS YOU into the present. The greater your gratitude, the fuller and more joyful, comforting, and comforted is your present. Brother David Steindl-Rast said, "As I express my gratitude, I become more deeply aware of it. And the greater my awareness, the greater my need to express it. What happens here is a spiraling ascent, a process of growth in ever expanding circles around a steady center."

Paul put the centrality of giving thanks this way: "Be joyful always; pray continually; give thanks in all circumstances, for this is God's will for you in Christ Jesus" (1 Thess 5:16–18 NIV).

Gratitude has enormous benefits. Among them, giving thanks:

1. Unlocks and unleashes a kind of spiritual energy that cannot be accessed other than by means of giving thanks. The end result: a state of "gratitude" or "gratefulness." Gratitude promotes peace, comfort, and life satisfaction.

2. Opens the heart and mind to the present and the world around you.

3. Tenderizes the heart and prepares it to receive joy and risk love.

4. Generates the sense of personal well-being and that things are as they should be, that ultimately everything will be alright, eternally.

5. Spurs on and strengthens faith and hope.

6. Diminishes boredom, cynicism, and skepticism.

7. Alleviates depression, suffering, and burnout.

And even though you may not have the power to instantly become grateful or to feel gratitude, as if turning on a light switch, you can nevertheless always give thanks by word and deed. The amazing thing is, the sheer act of giving of thanks by word and deed for the good you have, will actually generate gratitude. That is, your voicing and acting out of gratitude, while focusing on positive elements of your life, be they seemingly few in number, will of itself generate a sense of gratitude.

So just give thanks. As medieval mystic Meister Eckhart said, "If the only prayer you say in your whole life is 'Thank you,' that would suffice." And Albert Einstein said, "There are two ways to live your life. One is as though nothing is a miracle. The other is as though everything is a miracle."

Here is a breath prayer for gratitude: sitting comfortably, breathe in the gift of life-sustaining air. Then breathe out simple gratitude for the gift of life itself. Since the Holy Spirit is as the breath of God, image God breathing into you, as God did to Adam, and the resurrected Christ did to his disciples. Breathe in the gentle breath of God, silently entering your soul. Breathe out gratitude and joy for God's freely given breath of the Holy Spirit.

PRAYER FOR FORGIVENESS

WITHOUT FORGIVENESS AND ITS power to restore us and our relationships, we are destined to become hard of heart. And hardness of heart is anathema to God. The good news is that Jesus Christ brought God's forgiveness with him. Yet there is an important catch to receiving God's forgiveness: *in response to God's forgiveness, we must become forgivers ourselves*. Remaining unforgiving means refusing God's priceless gift of forgiveness. When you let in God's blanket forgiveness, you cannot help but forgive yourself and others, because of the freedom of heart and soul forgiveness brings. You do not want to hold onto unforgiveness any longer.

At the end of the Lord's Prayer, Jesus cautions us: "And forgive us our debts, as we also have forgiven our debtors . . . For if you forgive others their trespasses, your heavenly Father will also forgive you; but if you do not forgive others, neither will your Father forgive your trespasses" (Matt 6:12, 14–15).

Elsewhere, Jesus continues to connect being forgiven by God and with the necessity of forgiving others: "Whenever you stand praying, forgive, if you have anything against anyone; so that your Father in heaven may also forgive you your trespasses" (Mark 11:25). And: "Do not judge, and you will not be judged; do not condemn, and you will not be condemned. Forgive, and you will be forgiven" (Luke 6:37).

Being forgiving is a central characteristic of being Christian. Paul continues the instruction of our Lord: "And be kind to one another, tenderhearted, forgiving one another, as God in Christ has forgiven you" (Eph 4:32). Paul also writes, "Bear with one another and, if anyone has a complaint against another, forgive each other; just as the Lord has forgiven you, so you also must forgive" (Col 3:13).

Jesus breathed the Holy Spirit onto his disciples after his resurrection, along with the authority to forgive sins. Imagine how the breath of Christ must have felt on the disciples' faces. In this breath prayer exercise, breathe in Christ's forgiving breath, and accept God's forgiveness in Christ. Then as you breathe out, let go of all unforgiveness, turning everything and every-one over to God for God's justice and mercy. Let God take care of what is beyond you.

Breathe in with the word, "forgiven" (by God). And breathe out with the word, "forgiving" (by yourself). The truth is, you have to let in God's forgiveness before you can truly become forgiving. And that includes not only forgiving those who have wounded you, but also forgiving yourself as well. Many of us have greater difficulty forgiving ourselves than we do forgiving others. Forgive yourself as God in Christ has already forgiven you.

PRAYER FOR SILENCE

THIS NEXT BREATH PRAYER may seem at first a bit strange and difficult, but I assure you it works. I invite you to breathe in and out something we all need, but most of us do not get enough of: *silence*. Breathe in silence, and breathe out silence. And while doing so, listen to the subtle sound of your breath, drawing in and out like soft waves along the shoreline of your consciousness. Let go of all thoughts as they arise; let them be to you like silent seagulls taking flight along the shore, but not penetrating the water of your consciousness. Rather, become fully present to your breathing in, for its entire length, until it is time to breathe out. When you breathe out, rest in that gentle release of air, remaining in the silence of its passing.

The truth is, there is always silence at your center, just as there is always silence between the notes of a musical score, without which a melody cannot exist. The melodies of life require spaces between the notes, where silence can do its magical work.

As you prepare for this breath prayer, meditate on one of my prayer poems, titled "Silence." It is built on Psalm 46:20: "Be still, and know that I am God!"

Only through silence may you at last settle down, to hear what cannot be spoken; which may be grasped only in silence.

Silence carries truth undisturbed by sound.

Silence renders you vulnerable to self and Other discovery.

Silence like sonar is able to scan the shapes of the hidden, seeking to be known, finally, fully, as what it is, without the coloration of language.

Silence expands time, transferring it into simple duration, unmasked, unmeasured, unsecured.

Silence opens you to the time between the seconds, to the depths unrealizable in the multitude of surface tracks sound seduces your attention towards.

You may attend to the hearing or to the feeling, but not to both at the same time.

Only in silence may you hear what you truly feel.

Only in silence may you sense the God who is sensing you.

Your soul is surprisingly deep, like a mostly unexplored inland sea. And the deeper you go, the more silent becomes your inner being. It does not matter how much sound is going on around you or even within you. Your silent center still abides, as does God, awaiting your silence to sense God's silent presence.

PRAYER FOR LETTING GOD AND LETTING GO

WHEN ASKED THE QUESTION about where God is, an ancient sage said simply, "God is wherever we let God in." There is great truth here. We actually have to invite God in, rather than expect that God will do what we want without our asking or awareness. Who among us would enter into the home of a friend without first knocking and waiting for them to open the door?

When Jesus sent seventy disciples into the countryside to prepare the people for his coming, he said, "Whatever house you enter, first say, 'Peace to this house!' And if anyone is there who shares in peace, your peace will rest on that person; but if not, it will return to you. Remain in the same house, eating and drinking whatever they provide, for the laborer deserves to be paid. Do not move about from house to house" (Luke 10:5–7).

In other words, those who were open to and welcoming of the peace of Christ, were also ready for the coming of Jesus into their home and life. And those who were not open missed out on the all too rare moment of God's visitation. We do not know when God will arrive at our door, but we are cautioned to be ready, open, inviting, and welcoming.

I seek to be ready daily, and I have vowed to God:

I will be ready for you when you come. I do not know when you are coming or how, or where I will be, but I will be ready for you when you come.

I am not ready for you now, though I have been ready before. And I will be ready for you when you come.

God is always ready for you, even if you are not ready for God. These insistent words of Christ address me every time I pray: "Listen! I am standing at the door, knocking; if you hear my voice and open the door, I will come in to you and eat with you, and you with me" (Rev 3:20).

Sit in a comfortable straight-back chair, with both feet on the ground and hands resting on your thighs. Relax and practice "belly breathing," with your eyes closed. As you breathe in, let God in, so to say. And as you breathe out, let go and let God; that is, give your heart and soul and life to the God whom you have invited in, including all of your worries, fears, and concerns.

Breathe in, "Let God," and breathe out, "Let go." Do this for five to ten minutes. God is ever so gentle and kind. I assure you, whatever you give to God, God will take. Whatever of yourself you open to God, God will enter.

THE JESUS PRAYER

THE MOST SIGNIFICANT PRAYER in Eastern Orthodox Christianity is called the Jesus Prayer or also the Prayer of the Heart. What you do, just like a breath prayer, is to inhale the first half of a single sentence, and then exhale the remainder. The most commonly used and shortened form of this prayer: "Lord Jesus Christ, have mercy on me."

The scriptural basis for this ancient prayer, which goes back to at least the year 600, is likely this parable of Jesus:

> He also told this parable to some who trusted in themselves that they were righteous and regarded others with contempt: "Two men went up to the temple to pray, one a Pharisee and the other a tax collector. The Pharisee, standing by himself, was praying thus, 'God, I thank you that I am not like other people: thieves, rogues, adulterers, or even like this tax collector. I fast twice a week; I give a tenth of all my income.' But the tax collector, standing far off, would not even look up to heaven, but was beating his breast and saying, 'God, be merciful to me, a sinner!' I tell you, this man went down to his home justified rather than the other; for all who exalt themselves will be humbled, but all who humble themselves will be exalted." (Luke 18:9–14)

Pray the prayer like this: breathe in "Lord Jesus Christ," letting the words sink into your heart; then exhale, "have mercy on me." Imagine Jesus standing before you in his gentle, humble beauty; just let him into your heart. Breathe in his love, goodwill, and mercy. And when you exhale, imagine Christ's mercy flowing over all that you are, washing away whatever wounds, obstacles, and impurities you offer up, as you yield yourself to the merciful Lord of your life.

Silently repeat these words with every breath you take. After a time, these words and your heart will meld and you will find yourself in a better spiritual place. Over time and practice, you will not have to think about praying the prayer; the words will have become a rhythmic part of your breathing. No matter where you are or what you are doing, you can almost hear yourself quietly reciting these words. The effect can be significant, even mystical, bringing you the sensed presence of Jesus Christ, who not only has mercy, but above all, love for you.

PRAYING THE SCRIPTURES

"Your word is a lamp to my feet and a light to my path."
(Ps 119:105)

"Lectio Divina is an opportunity to slow down and experience God's Word deeply. An opportunity to savor the words of Scripture, to sit at God's table, to be nourished, fed and refreshed. An invitation to be fully present with our holy God."
—CINDEE SNIDER RE

"Seek in reading and you will find in meditation; knock in prayer and it will open to you in contemplation."
—ST. JOHN OF THE CROSS

HOW TO PRAY THE SCRIPTURES

THE SCRIPTURES ARE MEANT to be prayed as well as read. The process of praying the Scriptures (*Lectio Divina*) is time-honored, and has been practiced continuously for more than fifteen centuries in monastic communities. It consists of four essential cyclical steps or stages, which you may go back through repeatedly during a prayer session.

The Process:

1. *Reading*: Slowly read a brief passage. Truly listen and become fully present to the text. What does the text say? Read the text a few times, letting the words sink in.

2. *Meditation*: Reflect, ruminate on the text. What words especially grab you? What does the text say to you, mean to you right now?

3. *Prayer*: React, pray. What do you want to say to God? This stage includes your waiting for God's sensed presence, and hopefully, response.

4. *Contemplation*: This begins when you sense God drawing near, however subtly. It might be a calming assurance of God's presence, or a peace-bringing resting in God's Spirit. To release yourself into contemplation, you must consent to God's presence and action within you.

To better understand this fourfold process of praying the Scriptures, I offer the analogy of ordering food at a restaurant. First of all, you have to be hungry for food—just as you must have a desire for God. So how do you order off a menu? Through these four simple steps:

1. *Reading*: you first have to read what is on the menu. What is available?

2. *Meditation*: When you find something of interest, you will begin to ruminate on how it might taste and whether that is what you most want at that moment.

81

3. *Prayer*: You have to tell a waitperson what you want to order.

4. *Contemplation*: This commences when the food arrives and you begin to eat.

This really comes down to four questions you need to ask in order to pray a particular biblical passage:

1. What does the text say?

2. What does it say to me?

3. What do I want to say to God?

4. What does God want to say to me?

As a much needed example today, pray Jesus' compassionate appeal in Matthew 11:28–30: "Come to me, all you that are weary and are carrying heavy burdens, and I will give you rest. Take my yoke upon you, and learn from me; for I am gentle and humble in heart, and you will find rest for your souls. For my yoke is easy, and my burden is light."

THE HEBREW BIBLE

PSALM 23: THE GOOD SHEPHERD

PSALM 23 IS THE most popular of all 150 psalms. It touches most every spiritual base. And in tough times like these, it is just what we need to hear and quietly pray. And maybe memorize. It is personal, faith-building, and assuring. It is one of the seventy-three psalms attributed to King David, who was himself a shepherd of the sheep. To truly read and pray these words, we have to accept the fact that we are, after all, sheep. Like sheep we cannot see very far ahead of us; like sheep we can get lost and at times need help to get back where we need and want to be. And like sheep, we require protection from all manner of evil.

As you pray this great psalm, remember the four basic questions:

1. What does the passage say? (Reading)
2. What does the passage say to me? (Meditating)
3. What do I want to say to God? (Praying)
4. What does God want to say to me? (Contemplating)

> The LORD is my shepherd, I shall not want; he makes me lie down in green pastures. He leads me beside still waters; he restores my soul. He leads me in paths of righteousness for his name's sake. Even though I walk through the valley of the shadow of death, I fear no evil; for thou art with me; thy rod and thy staff, they comfort me. Thou preparest a table before me in the presence of my enemies; thou anointest my head with oil, my cup overflows. Surely goodness and mercy shall follow me all the days of my life; and I shall dwell in the house of the LORD forever. (RSV)

Note the shift from the third to the second person, in the face of potentially fatal danger. Now the psalmist says, *"for Thou art with me."* Many times in my life I have silently prayed these calming words, especially during my time in the Marine Corps.

The work of the shepherd is threefold. The shepherd *guides, nourishes,* and *protects* his sheep. As Psalm 23 attests, the Lord gives us rest, restores us, keeps us on the right path—because of who God is, rather than who we are—grants us peace and confidence in the face of death and opposition, loves us overmuch, and will be with us unto eternal life.

Jesus Christ, who is our Good Shepherd, gives us all of the above. He said:

> I am the good shepherd. The good shepherd lays down his life for the sheep . . . I am the good shepherd. I know my own and my own know me . . . My sheep hear my voice. I know them, and they follow me. I give them eternal life, and they will never perish. No one will snatch them out of my hand. What my Father has given me is greater than all else, and no one can snatch it out of the Father's hand. The Father and I are one. (John 10:11, 14, 27–30)

Note that the first sentence can also serve as a breath prayer. You can breathe in "The LORD is my Shepherd" and breathe out, "I shall not want."

PSALM 27: DO NOT FEAR

NOT ONLY IS THERE little knowledge of God in our land today; there is also much fear. And these two facts are deeply interconnected. Just imagine the marvelous consequences which would come to you if you could say, with comforted conviction, the following three verses. They are words of great faith and attest to the courage faith bestows:

> The LORD is my light and my salvation; whom shall I fear? The
> LORD is the stronghold of my life; of whom shall I be afraid? . . .
> I believe that I shall see the goodness of the LORD in the land of
> the living. Wait for the LORD; be strong, and let your heart take
> courage; wait for the LORD! (Ps 27:1, 13–14)

I well remember a dream I had back in my twenties, not long after the Holy Spirit first touched me, changing my life forever. It was the dream's final moment that mattered. As I looked at a blank and colorless wall, a holy hand began to write a sentence on that wall, while at the same time a heavenly voice strongly intoned that sentence directly to me: "Do not fear another day in your life!" I awoke immediately and knew it was of God. I also knew how difficult it would be to successfully live out of that command. And it surely has been.

Yet that is a sentence all Christians should live out of. On hundreds of occasions, while conducting a funeral, when unvoiced fear hovered sensed but not seen, I have quoted these words of Jesus, among the most comforting ever spoken. He said, just before he died for us:

> Do not let your hearts be troubled. Believe in God, believe also
> in me. In my Father's house there are many dwelling places. If
> it were not so, would I have told you that I go to prepare a place
> for you? And if I go and prepare a place for you, I will come
> again and will take you to myself, so that where I am, there you
> may be also . . . Peace I leave with you; my peace I give to you. I

do not give to you as the world gives. Do not let your hearts be troubled, and do not let them be afraid. (John 14:1–3, 27)

The "peace of Christ," which we need in abundance today, is the faith knowledge that everything will be alright, eternally. As John Lennon reportedly said: "Everything will be alright in the end. If things are not alright, it is not yet the end."

PSALM 37:1–11: WAIT FOR THE LORD

ONE OF THE MAJOR themes of the Hebrew Bible is the necessity of waiting for the Lord. This is something most all of us have or will go through during our lifetime. We will be forced to wait for God when something needs to happen that only God can accomplish.

Nowhere in the Bible is the centrality of waiting for God more powerfully stated than in Psalm 37. The psalmist urges us not to give up on our waiting, and promises that those who wait will finally be blessed by God in God's time and way. Somehow our not giving up turns out to be essential to our receiving what God intended to give us all along. Our waiting for God seems to have actually been a necessary stage in preparing us to receive at long last the well-being now and forever intended by God. Great words, these:

> Do not fret because of the wicked; do not be envious of wrongdoers, for they will soon fade like the grass, and wither like the green herb. Trust in the LORD, and do good; so you will live in the land, and enjoy security. Take delight in the LORD, and he will give you the desires of your heart. Commit your way to the LORD; trust in him, and he will act. He will make your vindication shine like the light, and the justice of your cause like the noonday.
>
> Be still before the LORD, and wait patiently for him; do not fret over those who prosper in their way, over those who carry out evil devices. Refrain from anger, and forsake wrath. Do not fret—it leads only to evil. For the wicked shall be cut off, but those who wait for the LORD shall inherit the land. Yet a little while, and the wicked will be no more; though you look diligently for their place, they will not be there. But the meek shall inherit the land, and delight themselves in abundant prosperity. (Ps 37:1–11)

I am convinced that the time spent waiting for God, be it a month or decade or even an entire lifetime, secretly strengthens us to continue abiding in and with God, once the living waters of heaven burst through to us and in us. What waiting develops in us is *steadfastness*, and with that the faith to continue believing *in spite of not receiving* the promised fruit of God's goodwill and way. Such was the faith of Abraham and Sarah. They waited over twenty-five years for God to finally fulfill the promise of progeny. Their faithful waiting became the model for our waiting for God in the steadfast faith that God will yet fulfill our heart's desire, above all the desire for God.

PSALM 40:1–3: GOD WILL SAVE YOU

I TURNED TO GOD long ago in desperation. My entire being shivered at the realization that without God, there was no possible solid ground upon which to build my life. Through a chain of events, I was becoming suicidal. An agnostic finally searching for God, God found me, literally saving my life. The first time I read these words of David, I wept in gratefulness:

> I waited patiently for the LORD; he inclined to me and heard my cry. He drew me up from the desolate pit, out of the miry bog, and set my feet upon a rock, making my steps secure. He put a new song in my mouth, a song of praise to our God. Many will see and fear, and put their trust in the LORD. (Ps 40:1–3)

That is just what God did for me, as God has done for countless others. And God can do so for you. In gratitude, I offered God this prayer about God's grace, which signifies an unmerited and undeserved gift, from a greater to a lesser person:

You did not have to do what you did for me: reach out and pluck me dying from the dark burning of boundless despair, from the mocking meaninglessness that exists apart from the light of your love.

You did not have to revive and restore me, living now for you, in the tender atmosphere of the Spirit between us, the gentle Holy Spirit of your love, which is better than life.

Why did you save me at the very hour of my going under, feeling then instead of the last wrenching of death's insensate claws, the first healing, knowing touch of your rescuing fingers?

That you, the living God, should be for me, who had not been for you; that you would reach out to hold and heal me, who can offer you only gratitude, and that inconsistently, inadequately, is the never diminishing wonder of my life.

That you did for me what you did not have to do, at the time when it had to be done, if it was ever going to be done, is the source of the ever-welling spring of life you birthed in my heart, the strength of my cleaving to you in hungering trust.

Nothing did you ask of me in exchange for your grace, no conditions or constraints did you set forth. Yet your lavish gifting aroused such ardor in me, such endless afterlife, that I keep on seeking to do for you what I do not have to but choose to do.

In saving my life, you gave me your life to found my life, your love to ground my love, your grace to spawn in me grace like light for others.

As best you can, open to the grace of God, who in Christ has come to save and succor you. Your salvation is not ultimately about you; it is about the Giver, God, who loves you as you are. Speaking for myself, I do not know of a greater miracle than that, the love of God.

PSALM 46: BE STILL TO KNOW GOD

THROUGH THE INTERNET WE are becoming ever more aware of dire events happening all over our planet, from the pandemic to global warming, conflicts to famines. Yet Psalm 46 assures us that with God as our one and only refuge and strength, we should not fear, regardless of outer circumstances. Rather, we need to be still to know and to trust the God who will save us. Talk about a timely psalm to pray:

> God is our refuge and strength, a very present help in trouble. Therefore, we will not fear, though the earth should change, though the mountains shake in the heart of the sea; though its waters roar and foam, though the mountains tremble with its tumult. There is a river whose streams make glad the city of God, the holy habitation of the Most High. God is in the midst of the city; it shall not be moved; God will help it when the morning dawns.
>
> The nations are in an uproar, the kingdoms totter; he utters his voice, the earth melts. The LORD of hosts is with us; the God of Jacob is our refuge. Come, behold the works of the LORD; see what desolations he has brought on the earth. He makes wars cease to the end of the earth; he breaks the bow, and shatters the spear; he burns the shields with fire. "Be still, and know that I am God! I am exalted among the nations; I am exalted in the earth." (Ps 46:1–10)

The key verse to let in and pray is, "Be still, and know that I am God." You can be more open and can take in more, when you are still. I remember a nun who led a time of silence and prayer during a four-day national prayer conference. Slowly she prayed: "Be still and know that I am God . . . Be still and know . . . Be still . . . Be."

This could become a breath prayer: breathe in "Be still," and breathe out "and know."

As I have written:

There is a knowing only stillness can convey, a grasping only silence will allow, so that insight may take root, dig deep, grab hold. Stillness is as essential to learning as sleep is to adjustment. Stillness permits time to expand just like space, so that truth may unfurl itself, and the knower unite with the knowing.

The heart daily yearns not only for calm and peace, but also for stillness and silence, so it may actually discern what it already knows, feel what it is feeling, release what it is withholding.

PSALM 51:10–13: WHAT GOD'S FORGIVENESS DOES

PSALM 51 IS MOST powerfully prayed when you truly seek the forgiveness of God. King David wrote it after the prophet Nathan told him that God knew about his joint sins of adultery with Bathsheba, now pregnant with his child, and the grievous murder of her faithful husband, Uriah. David did so in order to take Bathsheba as yet another wife. The psalm is David's confession, taking full responsibility for his actions, and seeking forgiveness and restoration.

While very few of us will ever sin against God's commandments to the extent of David, the psalm nevertheless has a universal message. All sin is against God, since "sin" comes from archery and literally means to miss the mark God sets before us on how to live right with God.

David admits his responsibility and throws himself on the mercy of God. In seeking forgiveness, he also seeks to go back to how things were between God and him before his grave sins. And these verses will speak to us as well, especially when we are in the throes of the dire consequences of disobedience of whatever sort. What David seeks is precisely what God's forgiveness can do:

> Create in me a clean heart, O God, and put a new and right spirit within me. Do not cast me away from your presence, and do not take your holy spirit from me. Restore to me the joy of your salvation, and sustain in me a willing spirit. Then I will teach transgressors your ways, and sinners will return to you. (vv. 10–13)

At one time or another in our lives, most of us will struggle with the weight of guilt, together with the felt need to confess our sins to another, such as a priest or pastor, which we are actually commanded to do (Jas 5:16; 1 John 1:8–10). That is why we have confession, and why Christ himself gave the church the authority to forgive sins (Matt 18:18; John 20:23).

At the close of the psalm, David realizes what is acceptable to God: "For you have no delight in sacrifice; if I were to give a burnt offering, you would not be pleased. The sacrifice acceptable to God is a broken spirit; a broken and contrite heart, O God, you will not despise" (vv. 16–17).

This raises an important question: where does God abide? As if in answer, God says, "I dwell in the high and holy place, and also with those who are contrite and humble in spirit, to revive the spirit of the humble, and to revive the heart of the contrite" (Isa 57:15).

And Jesus said, "For all who exalt themselves will be humbled, and those who humble themselves will be exalted" (Luke 14:11).

Sometimes it takes being broken, like David, in order to humbly beg for and be open to receive God's reviving forgiveness.

PSALM 63:1–8: THE THIRST FOR GOD

IF YOU GET THIRSTY enough, water is all you can think about. My severest thirst occurred during a practice war game in the mountains of Nevada when I was in the Marine Corps. After hours of hiking above eight thousand feet, my legs gave out due to the absence of oxygen. Along with that, I was out of water. While I was lying on the ground thinking I might die, another Marine casually walked by and tossed a canteen full of fresh water over to me. It was the greatest drink of water of my life. At that moment the curse of thirst gave way to the blessing of water.

We can thirst for God as well as for water. This thirst may be subtler and more difficult to define than the parched mouth of water deprivation. Yet once it is in operation, nothing and no one else but God can satisfy that thirst. Psalm 63 says this most poignantly:

> O God, you are my God, I seek you, my soul thirsts for you; my flesh faints for you, as in a dry and weary land where there is no water. So I have looked upon you in the sanctuary, beholding your power and glory.
>
> Because your steadfast love is better than life, my lips will praise you . . . My soul is satisfied as with a rich feast, and my mouth praises you with joyful lips when I think of you on my bed, and meditate on you in the watches of the night; for you have been my help, and in the shadow of your wings I sing for joy. My soul clings to you; your right hand upholds me. (Ps 63:1–8)

The thirst for God includes the thirst for meaning and purpose, peace and safety, faith, hope, and love, and all the fruit the Spirit of God alone can deliver. This is the water Jesus promised the woman at the well, including all who would come to him:

> If you knew the gift of God, and who it is that is saying to you, "Give me a drink," you would have asked him, and he would have given you living water . . . Everyone who drinks of this water will be thirsty again, but those who drink of the water that I will give them will never be thirsty. The water that I will give will become in them a spring of water gushing up to eternal life. (John 4:10, 13–14)

Pray for God to increase your thirst, in preparation for the filling and fulfilling water of the Spirit Jesus came to bring you, as freely as a Marine tossing over a canteen full of water.

PSALM 73:25–26: ONE-TO-ONE WITH GOD

AMONG THE MOST HAUNTING words of Scripture are those of Psalm 73:25–26. After the psalmist wonders why the wicked prosper, God shows him that they will be swept away at the end. Realizing then how ignorant and foolish he has been, and that God has in hidden fact been with him all the time, even holding on to and upholding him in secret, he realizes how important God is to him. He prays words which speak to me and to awakened humanity:

> Whom have I in heaven but you? And there is nothing on earth that I desire other than you. My flesh and my heart may fail, but God is the strength of my heart and my portion forever. (Ps 73:25–26)

Imagine God as the strength of your heart. Sense how intimate these words are, addressing God one-to-one, God having granted you permission to pray this way. What is more private than personal prayer? When you enter into your quiet inner prayer space, be grateful that what transpires is strictly between you and God. No one but God hears and knows and loves you in your totality, including your past, your present, and also your future. That God loves you now, means God, knowing the future, loves you forever, including the you who you are becoming. Embrace the faith that everything will end up being fine, eternally so.

Realize that God will be your "portion forever." I remember walking along a beach on the west coast of Florida with my wife some years ago. The sun was setting, and both of us were looking for interesting shells to take back to our home in landlocked Iowa. Kitty was about ten yards ahead of me. I stopped and looked west, at the glorious setting sun above the waters of the Gulf of Mexico. There was a shimmering path of slowly darkening rays of reddish orange seemingly between me and the sun, as if for just that moment the two of us were in a silent "I-You" connection. Then I looked ahead at my wife and asked her to stop and wait for me to catch up to her. Once together, we looked to the setting sun, and sure enough, she seemed to have the same one-to-one audience with the sun. Next I imagined what it would be like if the beach were long enough for all of humanity to be standing there gazing at the setting sun. We would each have our private moment with the sun, at the same time. So it is with our astounding God: we can and do have private audiences simultaneously with the God who is our destined portion, forever. How God can do this for us all is beyond me; but then, so is God.

PSALM 91: GOD'S PROTECTION

THERE IS SURELY NO grander a statement of faith in God than Psalm 91. It is a psalm to carry in your heart, especially when seeking God's protection from evil of all manner, including "deadly pestilence." As you read and pray the first ten verses, imagine how you would feel if you truly believed in and acted on these words. Imagine the peace, assurance, and strength these promises of God could generate in your heart:

> You who live in the shelter of the Most High, who abide in the shadow of the Almighty, will say to the LORD, "My refuge and my fortress; my God, in whom I trust." For he will deliver you from the snare of the fowler and from the deadly pestilence; he will cover you with his pinions, and under his wings you will find refuge; his faithfulness is a shield and buckler. You will not fear the terror of the night, or the arrow that flies by day, or the pestilence that stalks in darkness, or the destruction that wastes at noonday. A thousand may fall at your side, ten thousand at your right hand, but it will not come near you. You will only look with your eyes and see the punishment of the wicked.
>
> Because you have made the LORD your refuge, the Most High your dwelling place, no evil shall befall you, no scourge come near your tent. (Ps 91:1–10)

What does the psalm say is the key to your safety? *That you live in the shelter of God as your refuge and fortress.* This gets intensified in the remarkable final three verses of this psalm, which are truly soaked in faith. I will quote the RSV translation, changing the third into the second grammatical person, to render it more personal and powerful. I invite you to pray these two verses, as if God is actually saying them to you: "Because you cleave to me in love, I will deliver you. I will protect you, because you know my name. When you call to me, I will answer you; I will be with you in trouble, I will rescue you and honor you. With long life I will satisfy you, and show you my salvation" (Ps 91:14–16 RSV paraphrase).

Most significantly, the "cleave" in the original Hebrew means "devotion," signifying cleaving to, as lovers cleave to each other, or as parents and children cling to one another. The message? *Cleave to God and God will take care of you, all the way to your eternal life.*

PSALM 103:1–5: ON GIVING THANKS

IF YOU COULD START each day by blessing God, as if giving thanks for the mere rising of the sun—something we mostly take for granted—you would likely discover sufficient reasons for blessing God. The joyous Psalm 103 is like a celebration of the rising of the sun. As you pray these words, let them generate the four questions: what does the passage say?; what does it say to you?; what do you want to say to God?; and what does God want to say to you?

> Bless the LORD, O my soul, and all that is within me, bless his holy name. Bless the LORD, O my soul, and do not forget all his benefits—who forgives all your iniquity, who heals all your diseases, who redeems your life from the Pit, who crowns you with steadfast love and mercy, who satisfies you with good as long as you live so that your youth is renewed like the eagle's (vv. 1–5).

The amazing truth is that giving thanks with your mouth generates thankfulness in your heart. Expressing gratitude blesses you with the feeling of gratitude. Bless the Lord and you will discover how much you really have to bless the Lord for. If you seem to not be able to bless God for what you have, then bless God for what you do not have, that you do not want!

Rabbi Harold Kushner said, "Can you see the holiness in those things you take for granted—a paved road or a washing machine? If you concentrate on finding what is good in every situation, you will discover that your life will suddenly be filled with gratitude, a feeling that nurtures the soul."

And spiritual writer Ellen Vaughn said, "Whatever we are waiting for—peace of mind, contentment, grace, the inner awareness of simple abundance—it will surely come to us, but only when we are ready to receive it with an open and grateful heart."

You can actually choose to be open and grateful, because you have the God-given freedom to do so. The problem is that you just may not want to exercise this freedom. Strangely, feeling sorry for yourself can feel kind of good; whereas you might think giving thanks, while you do not have what you want, while maybe having what you do not want, is not being honest. Not so in spiritual reality. If you make a joyful noise to the Lord, don't be surprised to find yourself feeling joyful. Your action will actually precede the feeling. Feeling joyful is a gift of speaking and acting joyful.

PSALM 121: YOUR TRUE HELPER

IN AN EMERGENCY, WHEN you need help, sensing that you cannot make it on your own, that you are suddenly not in control of impending events, most all of us turn immediately to God for help. That is why it is said that there are no atheists in foxholes. Having been in foxholes as a Marine, and later serving as a chaplain in the National Guard, I can attest to that truth.

I vividly remember a cry to God for help late one November evening in 1961. An eighteen-year-old freshman, I was driving myself, my brother, and my sister back from Clearwater, Florida, to the University of Florida, after our Thanksgiving break. In the pitch blackness of a Florida night, they were fast asleep in the car, while I struggled to stay awake. As I approached an intersection, busy even at that hour, cruising over sixty miles an hour, I hit my brakes in preparation to stop. Nothing; the breaks simply were not there. And I could not pull off the road because it was a narrow two-lane highway with no shoulders, but with steep gullies on both sides. Though I was an agnostic at that time, without apparent forethought, I looked up at the dark sky and silently cried out "HELP!" to the possible "you" of a hidden God. Most fortunately, I crossed the intersection safely, seemingly between cars as if they were briefly parted, rather like the parted Red Sea, temporarily permitting safe passage for the Israelites.

Perhaps the most perfect and succinct biblical cry for help, together with a strong assurance of the protective presence and promise of God, is Psalm 121. Its eight verses say all that needs to be said in a cry for help. I suggest that after you read and pray it, you risk letting it in, and fully trusting in its majestic, peace-bearing words:

> I lift up my eyes to the hills—from where will my help come?
>
> My help comes from the LORD, who made heaven and earth.
>
> He will not let your foot be moved; he who keeps you will not slumber.

He who keeps Israel will neither slumber nor sleep.

The LORD is your keeper; the LORD is your shade at your right hand.

The sun shall not strike you by day, nor the moon by night.

The LORD will keep you from all evil; he will keep your life.

The LORD will keep your going out and your coming in from this time on and forevermore.

As Paul said, "If God is for us, who is against us?" (Rom 8:31b). Sense how absolute trust, together with an acceptance of being completely dependent upon God as your true and eternal Helper, makes you feel. Surely free from fear. Imagine living your life that way.

PSALM 126: GOD WILL TURN TEARS INTO JOY

ONLY GOD WILL HAVE the final word about your life. One extraordinary promise is that eventually, in God's timing and terms, God will turn your tears into joy. This is what the peace of Jesus Christ is about: all will be more than well at the end. Psalm 126 expresses this hope:

> When the LORD restored the fortunes of Zion, we were like those who dream. Then our mouth was filled with laughter, and our tongue with shouts of joy; then it was said among the nations, "The LORD has done great things for them." The LORD has done great things for us, and we rejoiced. Restore our fortunes, O LORD, like the watercourses in the Negeb. May those who sow in tears reap with shouts of joy. Those who go out weeping, bearing the seed for sowing, shall come home with shouts of joy, carrying their sheaves. (Ps 126:1–6)

This promise is also envisioned at the glorious end of the Bible:

> Then I saw a new heaven and a new earth; for the first heaven and the first earth had passed away, and the sea was no more. And I saw the holy city, the new Jerusalem, coming down out of heaven from God, prepared as a bride adorned for her husband. And I heard a loud voice from the throne saying, "See, the home of God is among mortals. He will dwell with them as their God; they will be his peoples, and God himself will be with them; he will wipe every tear from their eyes. Death will be no more; mourning and crying and pain will be no more, for the first things have passed away." And the one who was seated on the throne said, "See, I am making all things new." Also he said, 'Write this, for these words are trustworthy and true." (Rev 21:1–5)

What if God's healing will be greater than the wounds you suffer here? What if you will eventually praise God for the tears that made possible your joy? What if the healing salve of the Holy Spirit, once it caresses your painful brokenness, will be so wonderful that you will give thanks to God for the pain which made possible your ecstasy?

Though we will have to wait until heaven to know for certain, this is my faith, which I hold tightly, close to my heart. Risk faith; and hold these words close to your heart in prayer.

PSALM 131: REST IN GOD'S ARMS

THERE IS A LOT of fear out there these days, as we face a multitude of problems, from the pandemic to economic survival. It is difficult not to focus on the "what-if" or "could-be" variety of negative "possibility thinking" which our flesh is heir to. Anxiety has been defined as "living in the gap between the now and the then." So, are you living in the gaps? This wonderful little psalm seeks to resolve any and all fear. The shortest of all 150 psalms, Psalm 131 consists of a mere three verses:

> O LORD, my heart is not lifted up, my eyes are not raised too high; I do not occupy myself with things too great and too marvelous for me. But I have calmed and quieted my soul, like a weaned child with its mother; my soul is like the weaned child that is with me. O Israel, hope in the LORD from this time on and forevermore. (Ps 131:1–3)

Why occupy yourself with the great questions, such as: "Who am I?" "What is the meaning of life?" "What came before and what will come after this life?" These are really unanswerable questions, the answers to which are better left to God. As the Beatles song put it, words which I have quoted to persons in mind-numbing crisis: "There will be an answer, let it be." So the question is, can you, with God's help, "Let go and let God"?

Have you ever held an infant in your arms, whether your own or someone else's, and felt the total trust of that baby in your loving care? I have, with our three now-grown children and four grandchildren. Talk about living in the present moment. Holding your baby, looking with love at their precious form, life may not get better than that. And what do you want your baby to feel at that moment? Total trust, calmed confidence that you will take good care of that priceless life.

This psalm of David invites you to image God holding you as a mother holds a newly weaned child. As you first read, then meditate on, pray about, and finally wait for God's calming of your soul, accept that your ultimate Parent is in total charge of your being. Let go of the need to understand mysteries too great for you—or for any of us. Mystery just may be God's calling card. And your heavenly momma says everything will be alright, eternally. So if your Mother God says this to you, I assure you it will be so. Trusting in that will calm your inner child.

PSALM 139:1–18: THE SENSE OF GOD'S PRESENCE

THE AUTHOR OF PSALM 139—it is attributed to David—appears to have had an acute experience of God's nearness. I discovered this psalm while feeling all alone in a hotel room in a strange city during a conference for pastors. And these words made me feel known, connected to, and cared for by God. I have held them close to my heart ever thereafter.

Verses 1–6 address God's omniscience or immeasurable knowledge of us. Verses 7–12 address God's omnipresence or "every-where-ness." And verses 13–18 address God's omnipotence or all-powerfulness. Pray these verses together; be open to what God might say to you today.

> O LORD, you have searched me and known me. You know when I sit down and when I rise up; you discern my thoughts from far away. You search out my path and my lying down, and are acquainted with all my ways. Even before a word is on my tongue, O LORD, you know it completely. You hem me in, behind and before, and lay your hand upon me. Such knowledge is too wonderful for me; it is so high that I cannot attain it.
>
> Where can I go from your spirit? Or where can I flee from your presence? If I ascend to heaven, you are there; if I make my bed in Sheol, you are there. If I take the wings of the morning and settle at the farthest limits of the sea, even there your hand shall lead me, and your right hand shall hold me fast. If I say, "Surely the darkness shall cover me, and the light around me become night," even the darkness is not dark to you; the night is as bright as the day, for darkness is as light to you.
>
> For it was you who formed my inward parts; you knit me together in my mother's womb. I praise you, for I am fearfully and wonderfully made. Wonderful are your works; that I know very well. My frame was not hidden from you, when I was being made in secret, intricately woven in the depths of the earth. Your

eyes beheld my unformed substance. In your book were written all the days that were formed for me, when none of them as yet existed. How weighty to me are your thoughts, O God! How vast is the sum of them! I try to count them—they are more than the sand; I come to the end—I am still with you. (Ps 139:1–18)

Is your God too small? The God I have encountered is beyond imagery or imagination. And also more present than I can grasp. Take that leap of faith and discover just how present.

PROVERBS 3:5–8: TRUST IN
GOD WITH ALL YOUR HEART

ONE BIBLE PASSAGE WORTH praying and meditating on daily is Proverbs 3:5–8:

> Trust in the LORD with all your heart, and do not rely on your
> own insight. In all your ways acknowledge him, and he will
> make straight your paths. Do not be wise in your own eyes; fear
> the LORD, and turn away from evil. It will be a healing for your
> flesh and a refreshment for your body.

Back in August of 1993, my family went through what could have
been an unrelenting tragedy. We recited daily and held tightly to the above
Proverbs passage; and I am most grateful to say we discovered that from
everything God does indeed work for the good (Rom 8:28).

Not only are we to love the Lord our God with all our hearts. We are
also to trust God with all our hearts, even if that includes trusting God in
the face of inscrutable misfortune and suffering. Much of our daily lives may
be shrouded in the mystery of "why?" But this much is certain: you must
trust and love God with everything you have and are. And God will assuredly get you through whatever you may have to face or endure.

Biblical faith is as much *in spite of* as *because of* life events. The faith of
Abraham and Sarah, by which they remained right with God, was to believe
in God's promise of progeny in spite of enduring a twenty-five-year period
of barrenness. By the time the baby came, Sarah was ninety, way past her
ordinary capacity to give birth.

That was also the faith of Jesus, who suffered crucifixion as one seemingly abandoned by God. In his pain, Jesus cried out, "My God, my God,
why have you forsaken me?" (Ps 22:1; Mark 15:34). Yet he still trusted God
completely in spite of horrific circumstances. And look at the countless
progeny of Christ followers who arose after his death and resurrection.

One of my favorite poems in this context is "Faith and Sight," by Mary Gardner Brainard (1837–1905): "So, I go on, not knowing, /—I would not, if I might—/ I would rather walk in the dark with God / Than go alone in the light; / I would rather walk with Him by faith, / Than walk alone by sight."

True freedom sweeps through us when we trust in God rather than in our limited and limiting understanding. There is no better response to God's unconditional love for us than our unconditional trust in God.

ISAIAH 30:15:
RETURNING TO GOD

"For thus said the Lord GOD, the Holy One of Israel: In returning and rest you shall be saved; in quietness and in trust shall be your strength" (Isa 30:15).

It is never too late to return to God. I have witnessed persons returning to God after years of seeming alienation, for whatever reason. Perhaps it was due to suffering, and not believing that God was there, that God could or would save them from their painful state of helplessness and aloneness. Yet this single verse offers an extraordinary promise from the God of Israel, which God alone can fulfill.

Recently, a close friend, who had been an avowed atheist for decades, finally returned to God. He had to put down his beloved dog of fifteen years. On returning home, weeping, he discovered what he could not deny was a sign from God. His dog was to be cremated. And when he went to pick up his little dog's bed, next to his own, he found ashes both in the bed and all around it. There was no way it could have just happened. He sensed that it was a miracle, and came to believe that his dog was not only a gift from God, but had brought God to him. Broken by grief, he was at last open to the love God showed him.

The ancient rabbis said that whenever you turned or returned to God, no matter what your circumstances, you would have an immediate audience with God. Even if you did not feel it at the time, God would hear you and respond in some way. God heard me back in May 1967, when as an agnostic young man, sitting at a bar in Salt Lake City, I finally turned to an unknown God and asked for help. I finally, fully realized that without God, life had no meaning or ground. The following November, God touched me at a prayer meeting, changing my life forever.

Jesus came to call us home to God, regardless of where we were. He said, "Come to me, all you that are weary and are carrying heavy burdens, and I will give you rest. Take my yoke upon you, and learn from me; for I am gentle and humble in heart, and you will find rest for your souls. For my yoke is easy, and my burden is light" (Matt 11:28–30).

Countless good will follow your returning. You will attain a Sabbath rest with God, and in simple quietness and trust in the God who has saved you, you will receive strength for life.

ISAIAH 30:21: THIS IS THE WAY, WALK IN IT

WE WALK EVERY DAY, whether miles or meters. Our lives could be viewed as a very long journey along one or more paths, ways of living and being. On our own, it is surprisingly easy to get lost, to lose the sense of who and where we are. Then it is time to turn and seek the Lord, who is always there, and will not let us stay lost for long. The great truth is, there is no lost with God, only found. Turn to God in naked need, and God will find you. As I have written: "*Without you I am lost; with you I am found. To be found by you is eternal life, for you do not find only for now but forever.*"

After turning to God, let God's will guide you into the way you are to go. Your singular task should be to follow the Spirit's direction. In Isaiah 30:21, God said: "And when you turn to the right or when you turn to the left, your ears shall hear a word behind you, saying, 'This is the way; walk in it.'" If you do so, you will find rest for your soul. The path you are to walk begins when you seek to return to the Lord with all your heart. God also said: "Stand at the crossroads, and look, and ask for the ancient paths, where the good way lies; and walk in it, and find rest for your souls" (Jer 6:16).

This, in sum, is how to live with God: "Trust in the LORD with all your heart, and do not rely on your own insight. In all your ways acknowledge him, and he will make straight your paths" (Prov 3:5–6).

It is most significant that the early name for Christianity was "the Way." And the Way Christ calls us to walk is the path of love. Jesus commanded us to love one another as he loved us (John 13:34; 15:12). We are to walk in love. The apostle John said, "And this is love, that we walk according to his commandments; this is the commandment just as you have heard it from the beginning—you must walk in it" (2 John 1:6).

Walk in love, love for God and for humanity, empowered by God's love for you, and you will not only find rest for your soul. You will also discover that your strength really does dwell in quietness and in trust.

ISAIAH 40: THE COMFORT OF GOD

Nobody can comfort you like God. When the Spirit of God comforts you it is as your divine Parent. As God said through the prophet: "As a mother comforts her child, so I will comfort you; you shall be comforted in Jerusalem" (Isa 66:13).

Note that to comfort means both to make you feel better and also to strengthen you. We see this in Psalm 23:4, where the psalmist says: "Yea, though I walk through the valley of the shadow of death, I will fear no evil; For You are with me; Your rod and Your staff, they comfort me" (NKJV). The rod grants assuring peace; and staff strengthens as you follow God's sure guidance.

We behold the power of God's comforting with great clarity in Isaiah 40, when God announces to God's people in exile in Babylon that their time for comforting had finally come:

"Comfort, O comfort my people, says your God . . .

> Have you not known? Have you not heard? The Lord is the everlasting God, the Creator of the ends of the earth. He does not faint or grow weary; his understanding is unsearchable. He gives power to the faint, and strengthens the powerless. Even youths will faint and be weary, and the young will fall exhausted; but those who wait for the Lord shall renew their strength, they shall mount up with wings like eagles, they shall run and not be weary, they shall walk and not faint. (Isa 40:1, 28–31)

Jesus Christ came not only to save, but to comfort God's people. He said, "Blessed are those who mourn, for they shall be comforted" (Matt 5:4). And the apostle Paul said that God comforts us, so that we may become instruments of God's comfort to others: "Praise be to the God and Father of our Lord Jesus Christ, the Father of compassion and the God of all comfort, who comforts us in all our troubles, so that we can comfort those in any trouble with the comfort we ourselves have received from God" (2 Cor 1:3–4).

In these troubled, troubling times, let your heart prayerfully receive Paul's calming benediction, together with the comfort of God:

> Now may our Lord Jesus Christ himself and God our Father, who loved us and through grace gave us eternal comfort and good hope, comfort your hearts and strengthen them in every good work and word. (2 Thess 2:16–17)

ISAIAH 49:13–16: GOD IS ALSO OUR MOTHER

GOD IS NOT ONLY our Father. God is also our Mother. God is in truth our Single Parent. And we learn right away in Genesis 1:27 that both male and female are made equally in God's image: "So God created humankind in his image, in the image of God he created them; male and female he created them." That means the one God functions as both our Mother and Father. Through Isaiah, God says:

> Sing for joy, O heavens, and exult, O earth; break forth, O mountains, into singing! For the LORD has comforted his people, and will have compassion on his suffering ones. But Zion said, "The LORD has forsaken me, my Lord has forgotten me." Can a woman forget her nursing child, or show no compassion for the child of her womb? Even these may forget, yet I will not forget you. See, I have inscribed you on the palms of my hands; your walls are continually before me . . . As a mother comforts her child, so I will comfort you; you shall be comforted in Jerusalem. (Isa 49:13–16; 66:13)

It is most significant that the word for "compassion" in Hebrew literally means "womb love." Rare is the mother who would reject the child of her womb. And the fact that we children issue from her is the basis for Mother God's compassion and unconditional, unending love.

In short, that means you can also pray to God as your loving Mother. Reminiscent of Psalm 131, Dorothy M. Stewart wrote a beautiful prayer to God as Mother:

> Settle my silly heart, good Lord,
> Hold me still in your motherly embrace,
> enfolded by your wings of peace and love,
> and total acceptance. Soothe me,

love me into peace,
like a weaned child snuggled
in trust on her mother's lap.
So hold me, Lord,
and let us enjoy this time together.
Speak to my heart if you will,
but most of all be present to me,
and me to you.

I know that our experiences with our mothers can vary as much as our experiences with our fathers, positively or negatively. So the question for you is this: which would be easier and more comfortable and comforting to pray to, your heavenly Father or Mother? Though God is both and yet beyond both, focus right now on praying to God as your heavenly Mother. See where God leads you.

ISAIAH 54: THE COMPASSION OF GOD

IT IS MOST FORTUNATE for us that our God is compassionate. The Psalmist says: "As a father has compassion for his children, so the LORD has compassion for those who fear him . . . The LORD is good to all, and his compassion is over all that he has made" (Ps 103:13; 145:9).

If you have to choose between God showing you empathy or compassion, choose compassion. Though both are vital characteristics of God and of humanity at our best, empathy is passive, whereas compassion is active. When you have compassion for someone, you want to do more than just feel for them; you also want to do something for them to alleviate their suffering.

We see this in prominent display with the ministry of Jesus Christ, when he walked among us. Jesus had compassion on the multitudes who were as sheep without a shepherd: "As he went ashore, he saw a great crowd; and he had compassion for them, because they were like sheep without a shepherd; and he began to teach them many things" (Mark 6:34). And later, Jesus fed the four thousand due to his great compassion: "I have compassion for the crowd, because they have been with me now for three days and have nothing to eat" (Mark 8:2). Jesus healed two blind men out of compassion (Matt 20:30–34). He raised a woman's son from death back to life due to his compassion for her (Luke 7:12–16). And in his parable of the Prodigal Son, Jesus indicated that it was due to his compassion that the father ran to his son while he was on the road home, and restored him immediately (Luke 15:20).

In all of these stories, Jesus was operating in complete unity with God his Father and now our Father. It is God who is compassionate beyond our grasp or measuring. God admits through the prophet Isaiah that he does hide his face from us, due to our failings and flaws, but that God's final word to us is nevertheless one of utter compassion. Nowhere is this said more powerfully and poignantly than in Isaiah 54:

> For a brief moment I abandoned you, but with great compassion I will gather you. In overflowing wrath for a moment I hid my face from you, but with everlasting love I will have compassion on you, says the LORD, your Redeemer . . . For the mountains may depart and the hills be removed, but my steadfast love shall not depart from you, and my covenant of peace shall not be removed, says the LORD, who has compassion on you. (Isa 54:7–8, 10)

May God's compassion for you arise on your heart, like the sun on the earth. And let God's loving compassion sink deeply into your silent soul/soil. See what good things God has secretly planted within you will break through to your consciousness.

JEREMIAH 29:11–14: SEEKING AND FINDING GOD

IF YOU WANT TO find God, you have to seek with your whole heart. I found the truth of that in my own life and search for God. When I was a philosophy major in college, I merely wanted to know whether God could be proven to exist. I discovered that you can neither prove nor disprove God's existence by reason alone. A few years after graduation, when my heart had been trashed and life seemed to have lost its meaning, I sought God with everything I could muster.

Though baptized at thirteen, I walked away from and did not enter a church for ten years. I did not know where or how to begin the search for God, only that I was getting desperate to do so. Then I remembered the challenging yet promising words of Jesus:

> Ask, and it will be given you; search, and you will find; knock, and the door will be opened for you. For everyone who asks receives, and everyone who searches finds, and for everyone who knocks, the door will be opened. (Matt 7:7–8)

I decided to trust in and act on these words of Jesus, with the risky hope of finding God. Months later, on November 17, 1967, in the basement of a Catholic church with a group I had only met a few hours before, the Holy Spirit touched my barren heart, opening a gushing spring of living water I did not know existed until that moment.

It was not until 1972, while in seminary, that I came across God's promise through the prophet Jeremiah:

> For I know well the plans I have in mind for you . . . plans for your welfare and not for woe, so as to give you a future of hope. When you call me, and come and pray to me, I will listen to you. When you look for me, you will find me. Yes, when you seek me with all your heart, I will let you find me. (Jer 29:11–14a NAB)

"When you seek me with all your heart, I will let you find me." What a promise! I have witnessed the truth of God's promise in the lives of persons I served as pastor. Much akin, Jesus said, "Blessed are the pure in heart, for they will see God" (Matt 5:8). "Pure in heart" means "whole" in heart. That is, it means your whole heart seeks God, not just part of your heart. It also means you seek God not for this or that gift, but rather to know God personally.

It is wholehearted seeking that leads to wholehearted loving, finally fulfilling the great commandment. Truly, to know God is to love God.

JEREMIAH 31:31–34: THE LAW OF THE HEART

JEREMIAH (650–570 BCE) HAD the sorrowful duty of prophesying to the people Israel that God was so disappointed with them that they were headed for a fifty-year "trial separation" in Babylon. The question arose: was God going to divorce the people with whom he had covenanted? In one of the most important passages of the entire Bible, God declares that rather than rejecting, God intended to establish a new covenant and a new beginning, much greater than the previous covenant:

> The days are surely coming, says the LORD, when I will make a new covenant with the house of Israel and the house of Judah. It will not be like the covenant that I made with their ancestors when I took them by the hand to bring them out of the land of Egypt—a covenant that they broke, though I was their husband, says the LORD. But this is the covenant that I will make with the house of Israel after those days, says the LORD: I will put my law within them, and I will write it on their hearts; and I will be their God, and they shall be my people. No longer shall they teach one another, or say to each other, "Know the LORD," for they shall all know me, from the least of them to the greatest, says the LORD; for I will forgive their iniquity, and remember their sin no more. (Jer 31:31–34)

The philosopher Immanuel Kant (1724–1804) said that he was astounded by only two realities: "The starry skies above, and the moral law within." Yet the question remains whether God has already put God's "Torah" or "Law" within us, or whether that shall be a future event. Either way, our destiny is the same: God will plant God's morality and how we are to live within us. And at the same time, we will come to know God personally, the least among us not less than the greatest. And not only that, but God will forgive us and remember our sins no more.

This is surely what the "Christ-event" signifies: God's forgiveness and the implanting of Christ and the Holy Spirit within us. In his final discourse, Jesus taught us about the Holy Spirit, saying, "You know him, because he abides with you, and he will be in you" (John 14:17). And perhaps the central theme of Paul's letters is the implanting of Christ into our hearts (Gal 4:19; Col 1:27).

Has God already planted God's law into your heart? You could ask God in prayer. Above all, rest assured that "it is God who is at work in you, enabling you both to will and to work for his good pleasure" (Phil 2:13). What God is doing or has done in you, will come to the clear, clarifying light of God's endless love for you.

EZEKIEL 36:25–28: THE NEW HEART

JESUS TAUGHT US THAT the greatest commandment is this: "You shall love the LORD your God with all your heart, and with all your soul, and with all your might" (Deut 6:4; Mark 12:30). Yet surely we all have difficulty fulfilling this commandment. What is God going to do about the fickle, self-serving heart of humanity? This may well constitute the most significant problem of the Bible, which brought about the great flood (Gen 6:5–6).

So here is God's resolution, first addressed in Deuteronomy 30:6: "the LORD your God will circumcise your heart and the heart of your descendants, so that you will love the LORD your God with all your heart and with all your soul, in order that you may live." God later promises through the prophet Ezekiel (622–570 BCE) to actually change our hearts. These words have long inspired me, renewing my hope for myself and for the whole of humanity:

> I will sprinkle clean water upon you, and you shall be clean from all your uncleannesses, and from all your idols I will cleanse you. A new heart I will give you, and a new spirit I will put within you; and I will remove from your body the heart of stone and give you a heart of flesh. I will put my spirit within you, and make you follow my statutes and be careful to observe my ordinances. Then you shall live in the land that I gave to your ancestors; and you shall be my people, and I will be your God. (Ezek 36:25–28)

"A new heart I will give you, and a new spirit I will put within you." This is God's mysterious promise to which I cling; this is the action God is working in me, as in others. God vows to give us a "heart of flesh," while removing our hardened hearts of stone. How and when God will do this, and what it will be like to finally be able to love God as God wills, remain cloaked in the silence of God.

A heart of flesh would signify our hearts at their most human. Second-century Christian theologian Irenaeus may have been right, that the "Glory of God is humanity fully alive." In the haunting final words of his book *The Earth Gods*, Kahlil Gibran has the main character prophetically say: "Let love, human and frail, command the coming day." Perhaps nothing has greater value to God or humanity than the love that springs from and abides within, a heart of flesh.

If you invite God to cleanse, heal, and renew your heart, Christ will enter and make a home with you (John 14:23). In astounding fact, Christ will join his heart to your heart.

HOSEA 2:16–20: GOD WILL BE YOUR SPOUSE

THE DESIRE FOR GOD intensifies the nearer you draw to God, especially as God also draws nearer to you. So if God were destined to become your Spouse, not just your Sovereign and your Source, how might that affect your prayer life? Well, according to the Scriptures, get ready, because that is exactly what the prophets say is coming, in God's timing and way. God says through Isaiah, "Your Maker is your husband, the LORD of hosts is his name" (Isa 54:1). And in one of the most amazing prophecies in the entire Bible, that is just what God promises through Hosea. It has been called one of the highest "mountain peaks" of revelation in the entire Bible:

> On that day, says the LORD, you will call me, "My husband" . . . I will make for you a covenant on that day with the wild animals, the birds of the air, and the creeping things of the ground; and I will abolish the bow, the sword, and war from the land; and I will make you lie down in safety. And I will take you for my wife forever; I will take you for my wife in righteousness and in justice, in steadfast love, and in mercy. I will take you for my wife in faithfulness; and you shall know the LORD. (Hos 2:16–20)

One of the most significant saints of all time, Bernard of Clairvaux (1090–1153), wrote at length about our ultimate destiny being a marital union with God, when the love between God and humanity will have become thoroughly romantic. In the New Testament, Christ is referred to as the "bridegroom" on several occasions. And in the final chapters of the book of Revelation, John said, "And I saw the holy city, the new Jerusalem, coming down out of heaven from God, prepared as a bride adorned for her husband" (Rev 21:2).

It is not of course as if this will ever be a marriage between equals! God will remain God, and we will remain human, though taken up into and united with Christ. We will love God to the full extent of our being. And even now, "your life is hidden with Christ in God. When Christ who is your life is revealed, then you also will be revealed with him in glory" (Col 3:3–4).

The wondrous truth is, you will become more richly yourself in this coming union, than you ever could have become apart from Christ. As Jesus said, "Apart from me you can do nothing" (John 15:5). Through prayer, you can commune with God now, giving the romance an opportunity to begin in this life. The ultimate romantic relationship with God will be consummated, as the mystics said, in the bridal chambers of paradise.

If you do not yet have that kind of passion for God, just wait until the Beloved shows up.

MICAH 6:6–8: WHAT
THE LORD REQUIRES

OUR GOD IS MERCIFUL and just. Both at once, without the one overruling the other. God sees what we do not see, understands what we do not understand. Perhaps there is real truth to the proverb: "To know all is to forgive all." That is why we must leave the final judgment of a human life to God alone. Jesus warns us in the strongest terms not to judge, and says that the measure we use to judge others will be the measure God will use to judge us (Matt 7:1–2).

Our God is merciful. God gave a self-description to Moses, which was subsequently repeated throughout the Hebrew Bible: "The LORD passed before him, and proclaimed, 'The LORD, the LORD, a God merciful and gracious, slow to anger, and abounding in steadfast love and faithfulness'" (Exod 34:6).

At the same time, "the LORD loves justice" (Ps 37:28), and "works vindication and justice for all who are oppressed" (Ps 103:6). Who but God can be both merciful and just?

What then does this merciful and just God require of us? The prophet Micah gives us a timeless summary on which to meditate and pray:

> With what shall I come before the LORD and bow down before the exalted God? Shall I come before him with burnt offerings, with calves a year old? Will the LORD be pleased with thousands of rams, with ten thousand rivers of oil? Shall I offer my firstborn for my transgression, the fruit of my body for the sin of my soul? He has showed you, O man, what is good. And what does the LORD require of you? To act justly and to love mercy and to walk humbly with your God. (Mic 6:6–8 NIV)

"To act justly and to love mercy and to walk humbly with your God." Succinct and beautiful. We too, are to combine justice and mercy—both at once. And if we are going to make a mistake, it needs to be on the side of mercy. Jesus said twice that God "desires mercy, not sacrifice" (Matt 9:13; 12:7). Rather than to seek justice, God requires that we "act justly." That is, we are responsible for acting justly, rather than being a judge. And not only are we to be merciful; we are to "*love* mercy."

Finally, we are to "walk humbly" with God. The word "humble" has its root in "humus," meaning "of the earth." As God said to Adam after the fall: "You are dust, and to dust you shall return" (Gen 3:19). So to "walk humbly with your God," means to be aware of who you are relative to who God is. It means to think of yourself less while thinking of God more, to be God-conscious rather than self-conscious in your unending relationship with God.

THE NEW TESTAMENT

MATTHEW 6:25–34: GIVE CHRIST YOUR WORRIES

WE LIVE IN VERY troubling times. There is much about which you can worry. Jesus offers you the best, if not the only antidote: trust in God, who knows your needs and will provide for you. Read and pray this as if Jesus is addressing you personally:

> Therefore I tell you, do not worry about your life, what you will eat or what you will drink, or about your body, what you will wear. Is not life more than food, and the body more than cloth- ing? Look at the birds of the air; they neither sow nor reap nor gather into barns, and yet your heavenly Father feeds them. Are you not of more value than they? And can any of you by wor- rying add a single hour to your span of life? And why do you worry about clothing? Consider the lilies of the field, how they grow; they neither toil nor spin, yet I tell you, even Solomon in all his glory was not clothed like one of these. But if God so clothes the grass of the field, which is alive today and tomor- row is thrown into the oven, will he not much more clothe you—you of little faith? Therefore do not worry, saying, "What will we eat?" or "What will we drink?" or "What will we wear?" For it is the Gentiles who strive for all these things; and indeed your heavenly Father knows that you need all these things. But strive first for the kingdom of God and his righteousness, and all these things will be given to you as well. So do not worry about tomorrow, for tomorrow will bring worries of its own. Today's trouble is enough for today. (Matt 6:25–34)

This is, of course, easier said than done. We can get attached to our worries. I remember an elderly woman with many worries whom I at- tempted to comfort. She, however, giving me a kind of "back off" look, said: "Don't you tell me not to worry! Nothing I worry about happens."

137

Worry can be given up only on a daily basis; and when need be, on an hourly basis, when you take that leap of faith, and entrust your life with all your concerns to God. This you can do, with the Spirit's help. As Paul said, "Do not worry about anything, but in everything by prayer and supplication with thanksgiving let your requests be made known to God" (Phil 4:6). And when you are able to give your worries to Christ, what follows immediately as a spiritual gift is the peace of Christ. As Paul concludes: "And the peace of God, which surpasses all understanding, will guard your hearts and your minds in Christ Jesus" (Phil 4:7).

Imagine Christ directly across from you, with his hands extended out toward you, as if to receive all of your worries. And there is immeasurable love for you on his face. Give Jesus all your worries; and as you do, you will experience equally immeasurable peace flowing through you, namely the peace of Christ, which passes all understanding.

MATTHEW 11:28–30: LET CHRIST EASE YOUR BURDENS

THE BURDENS YOU BEAR indicate how much you care. Bearing burdens is tough enough, but bearing them all alone can become literally unbearable. The truth is, a burden which cannot be shared cannot be lifted. The good news, make that the "God news," is that Jesus Christ has expressly invited you to share your burdens with him. Here is Christ's remarkable invitation:

> Come to me, all you that are weary and are carrying heavy burdens, and I will give you rest. Take my yoke upon you, and learn from me; for I am gentle and humble in heart, and you will find rest for your souls. For my yoke is easy, and my burden is light. (Matt 11:28–30)

In these most difficult times, you may be reaching the limits of what you can bear on your own. Perhaps you already have, and find yourself stuck, seemingly unable to move forward with your life. If so, turn to Christ and come to him, if only in spirit, will, and desire. Humbled by circumstances, ask Christ to lift your burdens, and be willing to let them go, to give them to God, to let Christ bear them with and even for you. It has been said that true religious faith begins when you finally experience your absolute dependence on God. Rather than negative, this realization is good news: now you will be open for the "good news" of God's lightening love.

Jesus Christ is there for us. He will take our burdens upon his shoulders, so we can go free, freely to the God who loves us and sent Jesus to free us from those burdens we have been carrying on our own. Jesus said, "You will know the truth, and the truth will make you free . . . So if the Son makes you free, you will be free indeed" (John 8:32, 36).

The "yoke" Christ asks you to put on, rather than becoming a burden, will instead lift and support you through the rigors of your daily life. The yoke of Christ is in fact the love of God, which will also direct your steps as well as uphold you. Thus does Jesus say his yoke is "easy" and his burden is "light."

What are your burdens? List them to Christ and place them before him. Then calmly and gently humble yourself before the humble one. Brushing aside pride, ask Christ either to lift your burdens off of you—if you are willing to let Christ take them—or to bear them with you, and if need be, for you. Finally, trusting the Lord with all your heart, and embracing the freedom of Christ's yoke of love, you will at last find rest for your soul.

MATTHEW 13:44–46: THE HIDDEN TREASURE

MANY PERSONS THINK THAT being a Christian is about what you have to give up, rather than what treasure you might receive. Yet the truth is, what may appear as a sacrifice from the outside, will in fact be anything but a sacrifice from the inside, for the persons making it. Does God seek sacrifice from us? Are we supposed to get rid of all our possessions, so that we may possess the kingdom of heaven, whatever and whenever that is? God says through the prophet Hosea that God desires "steadfast love and not sacrifice, the knowledge of God rather than burnt offerings" (Hos 6:6). Jesus slightly amends this, telling his listeners, "Go and learn what this means, 'I desire mercy, not sacrifice'" (Matt 9:13).

For an important example, to those looking from the outside, what a couple does and willingly gives up after falling in love may appear foolish and immature. Yet it is anything but that to the couple. I remember two white-haired persons in their seventies, whose spouses had died a few years before. They met and fell in love on a cruise ship. In their unexpected romantic love, it was as if they returned to their young adult stage of wide-eyed optimism and sheer joy in each other. Being around them was a pure delight; they were truly in love. I know, because I got to conduct their pre-marriage counseling and perform their marriage ceremony. They ended up having nearly twenty years together, and I conducted their funerals a mere two months apart.

My point is this: when you fall in love, you will do whatever is necessary to enter fully into and fulfill that love. At that time, giving up singleness and independent living is not a sacrifice but a joy. The same dynamic holds true for Christians. As Paul said, "But we have this treasure in clay jars, so that it may be made clear that this extraordinary power belongs to God and does not come from us" (2 Cor 4:7). Who would guess from the outside the treasure that is ours on the inside?

Jesus puts this together in two brief parables:

> The kingdom of heaven is like treasure hidden in a field, which someone found and hid; then in his joy he goes and sells all that he has and buys that field. Again, the kingdom of heaven is like a merchant in search of fine pearls; on finding one pearl of great value, he went and sold all that he had and bought it. (Matt 13:44–46)

LUKE 10:38–42: THE ONE THING NEEDED

ONE OF THE GREAT spiritual questions is this: what does God seek from you? The likely answer: the same thing your heart seeks when you give it the freedom to express itself: direct encounter with God, the ultimate and true Beloved. Nothing less than that will fully satisfy God or your hungering heart.

One of the most significant scriptural stories about priorities from God's standpoint occurred between Jesus and the sisters Mary and Martha. This passage from Luke became among the most important biblical justifications for monastic life through two millennia:

> Now as they went on their way, he entered a certain village, where a woman named Martha welcomed him into her home. She had a sister named Mary, who sat at the Lord's feet and listened to what he was saying. But Martha was distracted by her many tasks; so she came to him and asked, "Lord, do you not care that my sister has left me to do all the work by myself? Tell her then to help me." But the Lord answered her, "Martha, Martha, you are worried and distracted by many things; there is need of only one thing. Mary has chosen the better part, which will not be taken away from her." (Luke 10:38–42)

It is easy to get distracted from the most important thing. Mary no doubt followed her heart, and knew what that was: seeking the face of God. As the psalmist said: "'Come,'" my heart says, 'seek his face!' Your face, LORD, do I seek" (Ps 27:6). And how do you seek the face of God? Mostly through prayer. And indirectly, you can behold the glory of God not only in your private place, but also in the heavens, on flower petals, on the faces of children, and through God's sensed presence with the gathered faithful. Only let the main thing remain the main thing.

There is of course both a Martha and a Mary in each of us, both a worker of good deeds and a seeker of God. While both are essential, what good is the former without being connected to the latter? Too many Christians have reduced what is *most essential* for their faith to works, rather than to prayer and personal connection with Christ. This is equivalent to doing things for Someone they do not know, and may even fear meeting.

Preparing a meal is important, of course. But it is not the *main thing* for God. God seeks above all your turning to God with your whole heart, with your full face, seeking to face God's face. As best you can, do not get distracted by the demands of the moment. Be as Mary in preparation for subsequently being as Martha. Then you will know *for whom* you are gratefully honored to prepare a meal. Prioritize the better part, which shall not be taken from you, ever.

LUKE 17:20–21: HEAVEN IS BETWEEN US

ANOTHER OF THE GREAT issues, right after "Where is God?," is "Where is the kingdom of God?" This exchange between Jesus and the Pharisees addresses that question:

> Once Jesus was asked by the Pharisees when the kingdom of God was coming, and he answered, "The kingdom of God is not coming with things that can be observed; nor will they say, 'Look, here it is!' or 'There it is!' For, in fact, the kingdom of God is among you." (Luke 17:20–21)

It is significant that the preposition Jesus used to indicate the place of God's kingdom, *entos*, means both "within" and also "among" or "between." Both. Not one without the other. God's kingdom, which includes heaven itself, is not only "there" and "then"; but it is also "here" and somehow, "now." As I wrote:

Heaven is between us.

If you do not get that, you do not get heaven.

One day you will get heaven, hopefully while you are still here, to enjoy and prepare for the greater heaven, where nothing will stop the flow of love between you and God and those of God.

Look for heaven inside you, you will not see or sense it.

Look for heaven beyond you, you will come up short,

As there is no place to point at something beyond life's rainbows.

But fall in love with your other, or better still: fall in love with God, beginning with God's beauty of sight and sound, nature and music, grandeur and glory, and you will connect with currents not of this place,

But which will come across from the great Otherness and like a magnetic field, will hold you safe in Love's sacred space.

Then you will know and know you know that whatever else it may be, heaven is between you and God, and those of God.

And once that field of Spirit has been entered, and has embraced you, it will slowly transform what is within and beyond you.

Heaven is that final abode where what is between, within, and beyond you will attain Love's blissful union.

How would it affect your life if you sensed heaven *between* you and your loved ones? And right here and now, not just there and then? Surely you would grasp and be grasped by the sacredness of the present moment. Pray for that grasping now, while you still have time to fully love and be loved by God and humanity.

LUKE 18:1–8: PERSEVERE IN PRAYER

You find out a lot about yourself by how well and how long you persevere to attain what you desire. If God readily gave you what you seek in prayer, there would be no reason to persevere. Yet that would also mean that there would be no real development of your character and maturity.

In his parable of the Widow and the Unjust Judge (Luke 18:1–8), Jesus instructs us to persevere in prayer and not to get discouraged when God does not seem to answer:

> Then Jesus told them a parable about their need to pray always and not to lose heart. He said, "In a certain city there was a judge who neither feared God nor had respect for people. In that city there was a widow who kept coming to him and saying, 'Grant me justice against my opponent.' For a while he refused; but later he said to himself, 'Though I have no fear of God and no respect for anyone, yet because this widow keeps bothering me, I will grant her justice, so that she may not wear me out by continually coming.'" And the Lord said, "Listen to what the unjust judge says. And will not God grant justice to his chosen ones who cry to him day and night? Will he delay long in helping them? I tell you, he will quickly grant justice to them. And yet, when the Son of Man comes, will he find faith on earth?"

This parable is what the rabbis called moving "from the lesser to the greater." If it is the case that even this cynical judge caved in to constant appeal, how much more will God eventually respond to those who, like the widow, keep pleading for what they desire? (Of course, what you are praying has to be God's will for you.)

Paul persevered longer and suffered more than most any other early disciple of Jesus Christ. He described what he himself had learned the hard way:

> Not only so, but we also rejoice in our sufferings, because we know that suffering produces perseverance; perseverance, character; and character, hope. And hope does not disappoint us, because God has poured out his love into our hearts by the Holy Spirit, whom he has given us. (Rom 5:3–5 NIV)

By your perseverance, you are showing God not only what you seek, but also who you really are. And only you can persevere. God will not do it for you. But if you choose to persevere, God will secretly reward you with the power to continue doing so, until you finally gain what your perseverance demonstrated to God that you truly seek. Just do not give up.

JOHN 3:1–8: YOU MUST BE BORN FROM ABOVE

ONE OF THE MOST profound sayings of Jesus comes from John 3:1–8:

> Now there was a Pharisee named Nicodemus, a leader of the Jews. He came to Jesus by night and said to him, "Rabbi, we know that you are a teacher who has come from God; for no one can do these signs that you do apart from the presence of God." Jesus answered him, "Very truly, I tell you, no one can see the kingdom of God without being born from above." Nicodemus said to him, "How can anyone be born after having grown old? Can one enter a second time into the mother's womb and be born?" Jesus answered, "Very truly, I tell you, no one can enter the kingdom of God without being born of water and Spirit. What is born of the flesh is flesh, and what is born of the Spirit is spirit. Do not be astonished that I said to you, 'You must be born from above.' The wind blows where it chooses, and you hear the sound of it, but you do not know where it comes from or where it goes. So it is with everyone who is born of the Spirit."

The Greek preposition which is used here for "from above" is "*anothen*." The preposition *ano* means "above," and the suffix *then* signifies "from." Yet *anothen* also means "again." Either way, what Jesus is saying is that you have to experience God, the Holy Spirit must touch or enter you in some unforgettable way in order to enter into the kingdom of God.

Perhaps the best analogy for being born from above or again is that of falling in love. Falling in love is a life-changing experience, built on the addition of the "other" and what that relationship brings to your life. All that you are falls in love with all that your partner is. Like the John Legend song says, "All of me, loves all of you." The difference between reading a romance novel and actually meeting and falling in love is analogous to the difference between being "once born" and "born from above." Yet how can you fall in love with someone you have never met? And how can the once born understand the twice born?

When I have conducted premarriage counseling with couples who had been divorced from a previous marriage, I would tell them that they get to start over again, rather like getting another "at bat" in baseball. And I would remind them that we learn more from our mistakes than our triumphs. And that with God, you can always get another "at bat."

Now when you finally fall in love with God, it will be forever. And you will realize that being "born again" or "born from above" means entering this love relationship with God, which actually takes place in God, in the Holy Spirit who is Love.

JOHN 4:7–14: THE WATER OF THE SPIRIT

THIRST CAN BE A curse, at least until you are able to drink cool, clear water. Then you might give thanks for your thirst, due to the pleasure and joy of fulfilling that thirst. We can also thirst for God. As the psalmist said, "As a deer longs for flowing streams, so my soul longs for you, O God. My soul thirsts for God, for the living God. When shall I come and behold the face of God?" (Ps 42:1–2).

What is it like to thirst for God? It is like dwelling in an inner waterless desert. Nothing is able to satisfy that strange yet relentless craving for goodness, truth, and beauty. Jesus promises us the living water of the Spirit, which alone can quench the thirst for God. Christ's exchange with a Samaritan woman at Jacob's well should be slowly prayed:

> A Samaritan woman came to draw water, and Jesus said to her, "Give me a drink." . . . The Samaritan woman said to him, "How is it that you, a Jew, ask a drink of me, a woman of Samaria?" . . . Jesus answered her, "If you knew the gift of God, and who it is that is saying to you, 'Give me a drink,' you would have asked him, and he would have given you living water." The woman said to him, "Sir, you have no bucket, and the well is deep. Where do you get that living water?" . . . Jesus said to her, "Everyone who drinks of this water will be thirsty again, but those who drink of the water that I will give them will never be thirsty. The water that I will give will become in them a spring of water gushing up to eternal life." (John 4:7–14)

Later in John's Gospel, Jesus invites us all to drink in his Spirit:

> On the last day of the festival . . . while Jesus was standing there, he cried out, "Let anyone who is thirsty come to me, and let the one who believes in me drink. As the scripture has said, 'Out of the believer's heart shall flow rivers of living water.'" Now

he said this about the Spirit, which believers in him were to receive; for as yet there was no Spirit, because Jesus was not yet glorified. (John 7:37–39)

Christ is now glorified; the Spirit's living water is available. Lean into your thirst, ask in faith, and await God's assured infilling. Discover the blessing of the thirst for God.

JOHN 14:1–3, 27: THE PEACE OF CHRIST

IMAGINE WATCHING THE END of a movie, seeing how wonderfully things turn out. How would it be to see the end before watching the rest of the movie? Now imagine that this movie is really the story of your life, including your final destiny. The Christian faith says this: everything will end well, eternally. So if things are not well right now, it is not yet the end. No matter what you may have to go through during your life, your end in God and with God is absolutely assured. Jesus is the goal and guarantor of our blessed end.

Jesus offered us this assurance just before he died for us: "Do not let your hearts be troubled. Believe in God, believe also in me. In my Father's house there are many dwelling places. If it were not so, would I have told you that I go to prepare a place for you? And if I go and prepare a place for you, I will come again and will take you to myself, so that where I am, there you may be also" (John 14:1–3). This is the Christian hope and faith.

This is the reason why Jesus could go on to say to us: "Peace I leave with you; my peace I give to you. I do not give to you as the world gives. Do not let your hearts be troubled, and do not let them be afraid" (John 14:27). Note: only God can grant eternal peace.

Peace is fundamentally relational. That is, peace is always *with* some person or situation. There are two basic focuses of peace: this life and the life to come. The central peace offered by God in the Hebrew Bible is *shalom*, and it signifies a peace for here and now. As an accurate analogy: imagine tossing a rock into a stilled pond. The point of ingress will raise the highest circular waves, with each expanding wave being of less and less intensity, until the last wave either dissipates or reaches the banks. Just so, shalom is first a peace with God, then built on that, a peace with yourself, with your spouse, your family, your friends, your neighbors, etc. It represents both an absence of hostilities and an indwelling of felt well-being.

The peace of Christ is well-being for both this life, and for the life to come. The life to come will include an eternal peace with God founded on a unity with Jesus, who promised "that where I am, there you may be also."

You could turn this into a breath prayer: breathe in "where I am," and breathe out "you will be also." Let your breath be as an unbroken, unbreakable span of faith drawing you and Christ ever closer.

JOHN 14:1–3: CHRIST IS COMING FOR YOU

AMONG THE MOST COMFORTING words Jesus Christ ever spoke were those uttered shortly before he was arrested and crucified. As a pastor, I have said these words at nearly every funeral I conducted. Thinking of us rather than himself, Jesus said:

> Do not let your hearts be troubled. Believe in God, believe also in me. In my Father's house there are many dwelling places. If it were not so, would I have told you that I go to prepare a place for you? And if I go and prepare a place for you, I will come again and will take you to myself, so that where I am, there you may be also. (John 14:1–3)

I have mostly considered these words as referring to Christ coming to meet us *after* we pass over to the other side. But I recently suggested to a spiritual woman that she meditate on these words in effort to sense Christ's presence right now. As I said this, the Spirit informed me that these words also mean, "Christ is coming for you *now*, so that you and Christ can become one in Spirit in *this* life; and after that, in the life to come." That would mean salvation is a *now* event, inclusive of a vivid sense of a lived connection, an ongoing communion with Christ today carrying us all the way into eternity. The question then becomes: why put off until death entering into this endless relationship Christ offers today? Why not let tomorrow and today join together with Christ, in Christ?

Yet most Christians focus on the earthly Jesus who once walked among us, rather than the mystical Christ who is with us right now and forever. We do not absorb Paul's instruction:

> From now on, therefore, we regard no one from a human point of view; even though we once knew Christ from a human point of view, we know him no longer in that way. So if anyone is in

Christ, there is a new creation: everything old has passed away; see, everything has become new! (2 Cor 5:16–17)

We desperately need to encounter the mystical Christ of John and Paul. To know this Christ is to love Christ. And as Jesus declared, "Those who love me will keep my word, and my Father will love them, and we will come to them and make our home with them" (John 14:23). That means a home with you right now, not just in the future. Invite the Christ who has come back for you into your inner home, *now*. Do not put off until tomorrow Christ's availability today.

JOHN 15:1–5, 9: HOW TO ABIDE IN CHRIST

THESE WORDS OF JESUS are at the heart of his mission among and meaning for us:

> I am the true vine, and my Father is the vinegrower. He removes every branch in me that bears no fruit. Every branch that bears fruit he prunes to make it bear more fruit. You have already been cleansed by the word that I have spoken to you. Abide in me as I abide in you. Just as the branch cannot bear fruit by itself unless it abides in the vine, neither can you unless you abide in me. I am the vine, you are the branches. Those who abide in me and I in them bear much fruit, because apart from me you can do nothing . . . As the Father has loved me, so I have loved you; abide in my love. (John 15:1–5, 9)

This is a great Scripture passage to pray. What does it say? What does it say to you? What do you want to say to God? What does God want to say to you?

For me the key words are: "Abide in me as I abide in you . . . Abide in my love."

You may treat this passage as a breath prayer. Sitting comfortably in a straight-back chair, simply breathe in "Abide in me," and breath out "as I abide in you." Or shorten it to one word: "Abide." Hold tight to that word; and when distractions come, let that word bring you back into prayerful connection. And in between both your breathing in and breathing out, sense Jesus softly saying to you, "Abide in my love."

Have you ever asked a loved one to "abide in my love," if not with those words, then with similar ones, like, "Please remember today how much I love you"? Well, Jesus is saying something far greater: "Unite with and remain in me and my love as I will remain in you."

The focus of this prayer is on Christ and entering into a mutual life with Christ *during the prayer itself*. Such a prayer offers a pathway toward attaining what Christ fervently prays for all disciples: "that they may be one, as we are one, I in them and you in me, that they may become completely one" (John 17:22–23). Indivisibility from Christ signifies salvation now.

JOHN 17:20–23: ONENESS WITH GOD

IN JOHN'S MAGNIFICENT GOSPEL, Jesus completes his final discourse to his disciples with what has been called his "priestly prayer." It is intended not only for his immediate disciples, but for all who will come after them, unto the present moment. The import of his prayer is the oneness and unity of Christ's followers of all generations with himself and God the Father:

> I ask not only on behalf of these, but also on behalf of those who will believe in me through their word, that they may all be one. As you, Father, are in me and I am in you, may they also be in us, so that the world may believe that you have sent me. The glory that you have given me I have given them, so that they may be one, as we are one, I in them and you in me, that they may become completely one, so that the world may know that you have sent me and have loved them even as you have loved me. (John 17:20–23)

The "oneness" of God is a pivotal revelation in the Hebrew Bible. The central confession of Orthodox Judaism, to be repeated three times a day, is called the *Shema*, meaning "Hear." It comes from Deuteronomy 6:4: "Hear, O Israel: The LORD our God, the LORD is one" (NIV). It is followed immediately by the greatest commandment of all: "You shall love the LORD your God with all your heart, and with all your soul, and with all your might" (6:5). We are commanded to focus all of our love laser-like on the Person of God. Loving God draws us into oneness with God.

The astounding reality is that through Christ we are invited into the very oneness of God. Oneness means unity, inseparability, as Jesus reports regarding the Trinity. He said that God the Father is greater than he is, and yet that he and the Father are "one." He vows to send us the Holy Spirit, the Spirit of Truth, to be our inner Counselor and Advocate. In short, Jesus invites us into the Trinity of God: "The glory that you have given me I have given them, so that they may be one, as we are one, I in them and you in me, that they may become completely one" (17:22).

This means that though Christ is greater than we are, we will nevertheless be one with him. And to be one with Christ means to live and move and have our being in Christ and the Holy Spirit. Salvation signifies life with God, in God. Heaven is where we share God with God.

JOHN 18:37–38: GOD IS THE TRUTH

THE SEARCH FOR TRUTH is also the search for God. And vice versa. We see this clearly in the brief but haunting exchange between Jesus and Pilate, just before Christ's crucifixion:

> Pilate asked him, "So you are a king?" Jesus answered, "You say that I am a king. For this I was born, and for this I came into the world, to testify to the truth. Everyone who belongs to the truth listens to my voice." Pilate asked him, "What is truth?" (John 18:37–38)

When God draws near to you, so does truth. It is like awaking to an even greater reality. Imagine not being aware that you are actually asleep until you suddenly wake up and discover that you were only dreaming. Such is the experience of being awakened to God, by God. Then you know God's truth, and know that you know and cannot forget that you know, even if you continue with your daytime existence in this temporary abode we call this life, on this earth.

God *is* ultimate truth, and God's truths are imperishable. When God draws near, radiant light shines in the darkness, which cannot comprehend or overpower it. Jesus Christ not only told us truth, but *is* God's truth for us. Jesus said, "You will know the truth, and the truth will make you free" (John 8:32), and "I am the way, and the truth, and the life" (John 14:6). Jesus three times called the Holy Spirit, whom he came to give us, "the Spirit of truth" (John 14:17; 15:26; 16:13). The Spirit offers us calming clarity and affirming assurance in an anxious world.

When God draws near to you in prayer, God will indeed set you free from falsehood and fear. Among the truths which God will communicate to you directly, without the need for words, are these: "I am real and with you always . . . I made you and you are mine . . . I know you as no other . . . I love you as no other . . . I am pleased with you . . . I will never abandon or reject you . . . I will take you to myself, that we may be together forever . . . Do not fear, for I am greater than the universe and your future in me is assured."

God can instantly implant these truths into your soul with a mere breath or tender touch of "the Spirit of truth." Once you have encountered God's inviolate truths, your singular task will be to trust in them, as in God. And live your life as a light of God to darkened humanity.

ROMANS 5:1-5: THE HOPE OF THE HOLY SPIRIT

LET THE FIRST STEP on your path to God be that of faith. Specifically, faith that you have obtained peace and right standing with God through Jesus Christ. Take hold of that faith, and let it take hold of you.

Once that faith is in place, strengthened by the surrounding grace of God, you will be ready to face unshaken whatever may come in your service to God and love. Paul puts forward what to expect, in one of the most important promise passages in the Bible:

> Therefore, since we are justified by faith, we have peace with God through our Lord Jesus Christ, through whom we have obtained access to this grace in which we stand; and we boast in our hope of sharing the glory of God. And not only that, but we also boast in our sufferings, knowing that suffering produces endurance, and endurance produces character, and character produces hope, and hope does not disappoint us, because God's love has been poured into our hearts through the Holy Spirit that has been given to us. (Rom 5:1-5)

Paul wants us to boast in the hope of sharing God's glory, as revealed and offered to us in Christ. We are even to boast about the sufferings that may come in service to the Lord. Why? Because such suffering, with the hidden upholding of the Spirit, will produce endurance, and endurance will lead to character. Then in a kind of circling back, character will produce hope. And this hope will not disappoint us or fade away, because God's love will be poured into our hearts through the Holy Spirit, given to us, as we persevere.

Suffering comes to us all. Essential to maturing in faith is learning to withstand such hardships. That includes the faith that suffering will generate endurance. Truth is, without suffering we cannot develop endurance. And endurance lays the foundation of character. Here I think of the elderly persons I served as a pastor who were members of the "greatest generation." They suffered through the Depression and World War II; yet they endured. In so doing, they attained a quiet strength of character, moral fortitude, and clarity about what truly matters in life.

As you pray this Scripture, ask the Holy Spirit to pour God's love into your heart. Through God's love and the hope that it generates, you will be able to endure what comes with the faith conviction that you are destined to share in the glory of God.

ROMANS 12:9–21: THE PATH OF WISDOM

THE BOOK OF ROMANS presents Paul at his most profound. And in the twelfth chapter, Paul puts forward a truly inspired vision of the path of divine wisdom, of how to live in the world as followers of Jesus Christ. Each of these thirteen verses should be taken into your heart and meditated upon over a lengthening period of time.

> Let love be genuine; hate what is evil, hold fast to what is good; love one another with mutual affection; outdo one another in showing honor. Do not lag in zeal, be ardent in spirit, serve the Lord. Rejoice in hope, be patient in suffering, persevere in prayer. Contribute to the needs of the saints; extend hospitality to strangers. Bless those who persecute you; bless and do not curse them. Rejoice with those who rejoice, weep with those who weep. Live in harmony with one another; do not be haughty, but associate with the lowly; do not claim to be wiser than you are. Do not repay anyone evil for evil, but take thought for what is noble in the sight of all. If it is possible, so far as it depends on you, live peaceably with all. Beloved, never avenge yourselves, but leave room for the wrath of God; for it is written, "Vengeance is mine, I will repay, says the Lord." No, "if your enemies are hungry, feed them; if they are thirsty, give them something to drink; for by doing this you will heap burning coals on their heads." Do not be overcome by evil, but overcome evil with good. (Rom 12:9–21)

We cannot attain such lofty love on our own. As Paul also tells us, we will have the Holy Spirit to assist us: "Likewise, the Spirit helps us in our weakness; for we do not know how to pray as we ought, but that very Spirit intercedes with sighs too deep for words. And God, who searches the heart, knows what is the mind of the Spirit, because the Spirit intercedes for the saints according to the will of God (Rom 8:26–27).

Paul spends the most time here addressing evil and how to deal with it. To repay evil with evil means to serve evil, instead of God. Rather than avenge yourself, leave that up to the "wrath of God," who will repay. That means to trust in the final justice of God. And to do as Jesus also teaches: overcome evil with good. You can never overcome evil with evil. You must not let your means violate your ends: only love can bring about love's goals. And God's ends are one with love's ends.

1 CORINTHIANS 13:1–8:
GOD'S AGAPE LOVE

IN THE MIDDLE OF his setting forth the gifts of the Holy Spirit, Paul turns to the highest gift of all: love. But not just any form of love; rather, the love which comes down from heaven. The Greek term for this love is *agape*. It appears almost exclusively in the New Testament in the Greek-speaking world of this time. It refers to God's own love, which we are first to seek, and then to share it with others.

Perhaps the best analogy of *agape* love is that of pouring water from a large pitcher into an empty glass. If you do not stop pouring, the water will eventually overflow the glass. That is the point at which love becomes *agape* love: when you have received more love than you can take in, when your heart is overflowing. Like the best of all possible news, you will simply have to give it to and share it with others.

Paul's description of God's love is the most magnificent of all time:

> If I speak in the tongues of mortals and of angels, but do not have love, I am a noisy gong or a clanging cymbal. And if I have prophetic powers, and understand all mysteries and all knowledge, and if I have all faith, so as to remove mountains, but do not have love, I am nothing. If I give away all my possessions, and if I hand over my body so that I may boast, but do not have love, I gain nothing.
>
> Love is patient; love is kind; love is not envious or boastful or arrogant or rude. It does not insist on its own way; it is not irritable or resentful; it does not rejoice in wrongdoing, but rejoices in the truth. It bears all things, believes all things, hopes all things, endures all things. Love never ends. (1 Cor 13:1–8)

Paul says, if you are going to receive any of the gifts of the Holy Spirit, start here. Without receiving and living out of God's love, nothing else you can do for Christ will be of any benefit in God's sight. Why? Because you will have diverged from following the path of love, continuing instead to move in the wrong direction. Every gift of the Spirit must begin with, remain, and end in God's own love, an ever self-giving and overflowing love toward others.

Pray for this gift above all. It is the very love with which God has loved you from your beginning, and will love you forever. Imagine such an utterly unconditional, pure love of you. When this love Paul celebrates finally fills you, it will overflow your heart. And when your heart overflows with this love straight from God, you will greatly desire to give it to and share it with others—without conditions or counting the cost. *That* is *agape* love.

2 CORINTHIANS 3:12–18: THE GLORY OF GOD

WE MAY NOT BE able to see God and live, but we can nevertheless encounter the glory of God. We may sense God's glory through the heavens: "The heavens are telling the glory of God; and the firmament proclaims his handiwork" (Ps 19:1). And through the miracle of prayer, we can actually feel the holy heat of the face of God, gazing upon us as we turn to God. When God draws near, so does God's glorious warmth. God's unseen yet present glory ignites our hearts, making our faces glow. I have experienced this warmth of God, making my face glow with the indescribable light of the glory of God with us.

The face of Moses glowed from his face-to-face meetings with God. So much so that Moses would put a veil over his face to keep the Israelites from seeing God's glory. It would have been too much for the Israelites to handle, this immeasurable glory. As Christians, however, we are able to behold God's glory in the face of Jesus Christ (2 Cor 4:6). Paul said:

> Since, then, we have such a hope, we act with great boldness, not like Moses, who put a veil over his face to keep the people of Israel from gazing at the end of the glory that was being set aside. But their minds were hardened. Indeed, to this very day, when they hear the reading of the old covenant, that same veil is still there, since only in Christ is it set aside. Indeed, to this very day whenever Moses is read, a veil lies over their minds; but when one turns to the Lord, the veil is removed. Now the Lord is the Spirit, and where the Spirit of the Lord is, there is freedom. And all of us, with unveiled faces, seeing the glory of the Lord as though reflected in a mirror, are being transformed into the same image from one degree of glory to another; for this comes from the Lord, the Spirit. (2 Cor 3:12–18)

When you pray, ask for the warmth of God's glory to shine upon you. Peter, James, and John encountered a transfigured Jesus Christ, whose face shone like the sun (Matt 17:2). In prayer, you too can encounter the glory of God in the glowing face of Jesus. Your own face will glow in response. Even though your eyes will not take in Christ and his glorified form, your heart will receive and respond to Christ with you.

After encountering this light of God, embrace it and let work its wonders in you, in order for you to "shine before others, so that they may see your good works and give glory to your Father in heaven" (Matt 5:16).

2 CORINTHIANS 5:16–20: OUR NEW CREATION IN CHRIST

AMONG PAUL'S MOST CHALLENGING yet promising words were those of 2 Corinthians 5:16–20. To pray them is to enter into Paul's own life-changing encounter with the risen Christ:

> From now on, therefore, we regard no one from a human point of view; even though we once knew Christ from a human point of view, we know him no longer in that way. So if anyone is in Christ, there is a new creation: everything old has passed away; see, everything has become new! All this is from God, who reconciled us to himself through Christ, and has given us the ministry of reconciliation; that is, in Christ God was reconciling the world to himself, not counting their trespasses against them, and entrusting the message of reconciliation to us. So we are ambassadors for Christ, since God is making his appeal through us; we entreat you on behalf of Christ, be reconciled to God. (2 Cor 5:16–20)

Paul never met Jesus Christ during his earthly ministry. He first encountered the risen Lord on the road to Damascus, forever changing his life. None of us will ever encounter the physical Christ; rather, we may meet Jesus as a mystical person of inestimable power, healing, and love. To meet Christ is to meet God. I have encountered this Christ, and am in a permanent heart-to-heart connection. That union is what I understand Paul to be expressing in this passage.

If you have met Christ, you are not the same person as you were before your encounter. If you have not yet met Christ, who is destined be your eternal partner, your beloved beyond male or female, let that coming meeting ground your hope. The "new creation" is who you will be with and in Christ, when you will no longer be alone, even within yourself. And nothing will ever be able to separate you from the love of God in Christ (Rom 8:38–39).

In this new creation, you will be more fully yourself together with Christ, than you ever could be on your own. It is like falling in love: now you are no longer a single entity; now you have a divine partner in a new and endless life together. This love relationship will constitute your "new creation" in Christ, not a creation alone, but together as a unit with Christ.

And when this happens, you will greatly desire others to share this with you; you will inevitably become an ambassador of Christ's reconciliation and peace.

Do not fear the mystical Christ, for as Christ draws near in prayer, you will immediately sense that this is "the one," the true love of your eternal life—a life together.

GALATIANS 5:1: THE FREEDOM OF CHRIST

THOUGH YOU MAY AT times fear the truth, Jesus says that "you will know the truth, and the truth will make you free . . . So if the Son makes you free, you will be free indeed" (John 8:32, 36). And the apostle Paul echoes Christ's words, when he says, "For freedom Christ has set us free. Stand firm, therefore, and do not submit again to a yoke of slavery" (Gal 5:1).

At the heart of Jesus' mission was to set us free from every manner of bondage. In his very first message to humanity, delivered to his own people in Nazareth, Jesus quoted the prophet Isaiah (61:1-2):

> "The Spirit of the Lord is upon me, because he has anointed me to bring good news to the poor. He has sent me to proclaim release to the captives and recovery of sight to the blind, to let the oppressed go free, to proclaim the year of the Lord's favor." And he rolled up the scroll, gave it back to the attendant, and sat down. The eyes of all in the synagogue were fixed on him. Then he began to say to them, "Today this scripture has been fulfilled in your hearing." (Luke 4:18-21)

The freedom of Christ is a freedom *from* and freedom *for*. Paul indicates what this is a freedom *from*: "For the law of the Spirit of life in Christ Jesus has set you free from the law of sin and of death . . . For the creation waits with eager longing for the revealing of the children of God; for the creation was subjected to futility, not of its own will but by the will of the one who subjected it, in hope that the creation itself will be set free from its bondage to decay and will obtain the freedom of the glory of the children of God" (Rom 8:2, 19-21).

Paul also describes what the freedom Christ brought us is *for*:

> Now the Lord is the Spirit, and where the Spirit of the Lord is, there is freedom. And all of us, with unveiled faces, seeing

the glory of the Lord as though reflected in a mirror, are be-ing transformed into the same image from one degree of glory to another; for this comes from the Lord, the Spirit. (2 Cor 3:17–18)

Jesus Christ has freed us from all forms of bondage, from anything which would prevent us from seeking and finding God. He has freed us for communing face-to-face with the Lord, for being transformed into Christ-likeness. You will become like the one you face.

You can experience no greater freedom than in prayer. No one can stop you from praying or determine what you pray. Therefore, embrace your freedom; as you pray, feel the birdlike freedom of flight, in the limitless heavens of God.

GALATIANS 5:22–23: THE FRUIT OF THE SPIRIT

THERE ARE THE GIFTS of the Holy Spirit, which countless Christians have prayed for and received, especially over the last century. Then there are the fruits of the Spirit. God bestows the former on all believers for the sake of the common good of the body of Christ (1 Cor 12:7). The latter emerge from within believers when they invite in and let the Spirit work for the good of all. The "fruit" evidences the presence of Christ's Spirit working in and between us.

Paul names nine priceless fruit of the Holy Spirit:

> By contrast, the fruit of the Spirit is love, joy, peace, patience, kindness, generosity, faithfulness, gentleness, and self-control. There is no law against such things . . . If we live by the Spirit, let us also be guided by the Spirit. (Gal 5:22–23, 25)

In a similar statement, Paul sets forth how we are to live together as followers of Christ. Here we can sense the fruit of the Spirit in operation:

> As God's chosen ones, holy and beloved, clothe yourselves with compassion, kindness, humility, meekness, and patience. Bear with one another and, if anyone has a complaint against another, forgive each other; just as the Lord has forgiven you, so you also must forgive. Above all, clothe yourselves with love, which binds everything together in perfect harmony. And let the peace of Christ rule in your hearts, to which indeed you were called in the one body. And be thankful. (Col 3:12–15)

How do we obtain the fruit of the Spirit? Strictly through the empowerment of the Holy Spirit; which if we permit, will slowly turn us into true "Christ-ians." They are the fruit which come from being connected to, and in active relationship with, God. They are unmistakable evidence of the hidden presence of and participation in Jesus Christ.

Think of Jesus as you read and pray for these nine fruits of the Spirit again: "love, joy, peace, patience, kindness, generosity, faithfulness, gentleness, and self-control." The really good news is that you do not have to struggle to attain one or all of them; they will be in evidence when you permit yourself to be guided by Christ's Spirit. That is, they are gifts of God, rather than the fruit of your labor.

What is more, these nine fruit are all interconnected, like rare pearls on a golden chain of being. Receive one, and you will receive them all. This will happen of itself when you enter into relationship with Christ. So invite in and abide with Jesus Christ; then the fruit of the Spirit will be yours as well.

There is more. (There is always more with God!) What God works *in* you, God also seeks to work *through* you. How else can you join Christ's endless mission to be the light of the world? "Let your light so shine" . . . *so that others may want what you have.* Seek to bring to others what God has brought to you.

EPHESIANS 3:16–19:
PAUL'S PRAYER FOR US

THERE IS NO MORE powerful, succinct, and timeless prayer in the Bible than Paul's prayer in Ephesians 3, really for all Christians for all time. It is up there with Jesus' "priestly prayer" of John 17. It is a prayer of Paul's passionate hope for others to share with him in his union with Christ. Please read it slowly and reread it over time. As the words sink in, their meaning will magnify. And the further you get in the spiritual life with God, the greater will be their meaning to you. Every sentence deserves to be meditated upon, then prayed.

The four questions to be asked in praying the Scriptures really need to be addressed in this unique, unexpected, and confessional prayer. What does this passage say? What does it say to you? What do you want to say to God? And what does God want to say to you? Add to that: what is Paul seeing, and how can you grasp it?

> I pray that, according to the riches of his glory, he may grant that you may be strengthened in your inner being with power through his Spirit, and that Christ may dwell in your hearts through faith, as you are being rooted and grounded in love. I pray that you may have the power to comprehend, with all the saints, what is the breadth and length and height and depth, and to know the love of Christ that surpasses knowledge, so that you may be filled with all the fullness of God. (Eph 3:16–19)

Paul prays for you to be strengthened in your hidden heart through the Spirit, and that Christ may actively dwell in your heart. Both the Spirit's strengthening and Christ dwelling in your heart are real, actual, as I can attest from my own life. Christ being in you roots and grounds you in love, from which nothing can separate you. In that silently blessed union, you will finally be able to comprehend, as have the saints before you, what is the truth Jesus came to reveal and constitute. Paul wants you to know what he knows, namely the height, depth, and breadth of Christ's love, which surpasses human knowledge and language. At that vaulted point, God will have filled you with the very fullness of God, as the immense ocean fills a little bucket to overflowing. The way into this eternal fullness is through earnest desire for and faith in God.

Go for this in-filling now. Nothing less than attaining your destiny in Christ will truly satisfy you.

EPHESIANS 6:10–18: THE WHOLE ARMOR OF GOD

EVIL IS AFOOT THESE days. We see it first as an attack on the truth and our trust in the truth. Note that the evil one is the father of lies. Jesus warned us: "He was a murderer from the beginning and does not stand in the truth, because there is no truth in him. When he lies, he speaks according to his own nature, for he is a liar and the father of lies" (John 8:44). Christ alone is "the way, the truth and the life" (John 14:6).

Paul instructs us in how to face, withstand, and eventually prevail over evil, unafraid:

> Finally, be strong in the Lord and in the strength of his power
> ... Therefore, take up the whole armor of God, so that you may
> be able to withstand on that evil day, and having done every-
> thing, to stand firm. Stand therefore, and fasten the belt of truth
> around your waist, and put on the breastplate of righteousness.
> As shoes for your feet put on whatever will make you ready to
> proclaim the gospel of peace. With all of these, take the shield of
> faith, with which you will be able to quench all the flaming ar-
> rows of the evil one. Take the helmet of salvation, and the sword
> of the Spirit, which is the word of God. Pray in the Spirit at all
> times in every prayer and supplication. (Eph 6:10, 13–18a)

To flesh out Paul's vital instruction:

"Fasten the belt of truth around your waist." Hold tight the truth of God's love and power around your most vulnerable area.

"Put on the breastplate of righteousness." Remain right with God through faith and good living.

"As shoes . . . put on whatever will make you ready to proclaim the gospel of peace." First receive the peace of Christ, then offer it to all. Let your first step toward others be one of peace.

"Take the shield of faith, with which you will be able to quench all the flaming arrows of the evil one." Let your faith be as unconditional as God's love is unchanging. Trust God in spite of as well as because of circumstances.

"Take the helmet of salvation." Believe with your heart, mind, and soul that you are saved in Christ. This belief will protect your mind, and will become self-authenticating.

"And the sword of the Spirit, which is the word of God." Defend yourself by means of God's word, the Scriptures, as Jesus did against Satan (Matt 4:1–11). That requires Scripture study, best accomplished in a small group.

"Pray in the Spirit at all times in every prayer and supplication." Stay connected to the Spirit and let the Spirit guide you always. Cleave to the Spirit, and no harm will come your way (see Ps 91:14–16), except whatever God permits for the sake of your maturing and eternal well-being. Truly, what God does not protect you from, God will strengthen you through.

PHILIPPIANS 4:4–7: ATTAINING GOD'S PROTECTIVE PEACE

THE APOSTLE PAUL OFFERS us a remarkable step-by-step process for how to attain "the peace of God, which surpasses all understanding." These inspired words present a pathway to the protective peace of Jesus Christ:

> Rejoice in the Lord always; again I will say, rejoice. Let your gentleness be known to everyone. The Lord is near. Do not worry about anything, but in everything by prayer and supplication with thanksgiving let your requests be made known to God. And the peace of God, which surpasses all understanding, will guard your hearts and your minds in Christ Jesus. (Phil 4:4–7)

Rejoice in the Lord always; again I will say, rejoice. In the beginning is rejoicing, not just about anything in your life, but specifically rejoicing about and in God. When you rejoice in God, you will sense and accept your own humbled humanity. You are not in final control of your life or those of your loved ones. God is; and God in Christ has come to reveal God's love and offer of salvation. Therefore, rejoice in this inestimable good news.

Let your gentleness be known to everyone. Rejoicing opens your heart to your own gentleness, even tenderness about that for which you rejoice.

The Lord is near. Once your humbled heart is open, you can sense the presence of God. God dwells "with those who are contrite and humble in spirit, to revive the spirit of the humble, and to revive the heart of the contrite" (Isa 57:15b). God draws near to and exalts the humble.

Do not worry about anything. Sensing now the presence of God, you will realize that there is nothing to fear. Now you can rejoice with the Psalmist: "The LORD is my light and my salvation; whom shall I fear? The LORD is the stronghold of my life; of whom shall I be afraid?" (Ps 27:1).

But in everything by prayer and supplication with thanksgiving let your requests be made known to God. Rejoicing, humbled, sensing God's presence, encouraged to be fearless, you are truly ready to offer your requests to God, in the blessed context of trusting thanksgiving.

And the peace of God, which surpasses all understanding, will guard your hearts and your minds in Christ Jesus. After you have made your requests known to God, in your heightened sense of God's presence, a peace will descend upon you like a misty cloud, beyond your grasp or comprehension, which will silently guard your heart and mind in the Spirit of Jesus Christ. It is for you to continue to let God guard your heart, which is, above all, precious to God.

PHILIPPIANS 4:8–9: THINK ABOUT THESE THINGS

THOUGH IT IS NOT certain where Paul was when he wrote his most positive letter, he did so while in prison, either in Rome or Ephesus around the year 62. Paul succinctly tells us what to focus on for the sake of our well-being, as well as those around us.

> Finally, beloved, whatever is true, whatever is honorable, whatever is just, whatever is pure, whatever is pleasing, whatever is commendable, if there is any excellence and if there is anything worthy of praise, think about these things. Keep on doing the things that you have learned and received and heard and seen in me, and the God of peace will be with you. (Phil 4:8–9)

To a surprising extent, we tend to become like whatever we spend our time focusing on. Focus on the negative, and you will become negative. Focus on what Paul is suggesting and you will likely absorb and act out of whatever is excellent and worthy of praise. Such positivity will enhance your self-belief and willingness to actually do what is excellent and worthy of praise. *Positivity opens the gate to potentiality.* Negativity closes the gate to possibility.

We also tend to become like the persons with whom we associate. Be around positive persons who seek positive outcomes not only for themselves, but for others, and you will readily become like them. Be around negative persons, and it will, over time, darken your soul.

Here is a slight paraphrase of Proverbs 23:7: "For as a person thinks in their heart, so they are" (NKJV). As you think about yourself, so will you act *as if* it were the truth. This is called the "self-fulfilling prophecy." It states that we tend to become either what we expect ourselves to become, or what others expect us to become. As you see and think of yourself, so will you act out *as if* it were your truth. Then it will likely become *your* truth—but not *the* truth, as known to God. You have to draw near to God in faith, to discover God's truth for you, which will be good.

You also need to focus on what you have rather than what you do not have. A wise woman friend recently texted me something she lives by: "Any day I can keep my gratitude higher than my expectations is a good day." Start your day by focusing on what you are grateful for, instead of what you seek but do not have. As Paul says, such a positive mindset will prepare you to receive the peace of God.

The more negative you are, the more difficult it will be for you to accept the peace of God. But if you "keep on doing the things" as Paul suggests, you will assuredly embrace and be embraced by the peace of God.

COLOSSIANS 3:1–4: SET
YOUR HEART ON CHRIST

ONE OF THE MISUNDERSTANDINGS of many Christians today is that the benefits of Jesus Christ are to be received right now, today. This includes physical and monetary well-being for us and our loved ones. We want the payoffs for faith *in this life*. While there are definitely good things to be ours now by virtue of our faith in Christ and right standing with God, they can only constitute a *down payment* on the really good stuff to be ours, not the *principal*. The "principal" is Christ, together with our impending union with him. This will only be fully ours after this life.

This is all the more difficult for us today, since we do not readily accept or easily withstand "delayed gratification." Paul corrects our narrow vision in these dramatic terms:

> So if you have been raised with Christ, seek the things that are above, where Christ is, seated at the right hand of God. Set your minds on things that are above, not on things that are on earth, for you have died, and your life is hidden with Christ in God. When Christ who is your life is revealed, then you also will be revealed with him in glory. (Col 3:1–4)

What a strange thing to say: "your life is hidden with Christ in God." This sounds as if our life is hidden *right now*, with Christ, in God. Paul continues: "When Christ who is your life is revealed, then you also will be revealed with him in glory." These present-tense verbs are amazing. They indicate that some things have already transpired, even if you are unable to witness or take them in. This is rather like a "good news-bad news" scenario, when you are told that the Christmas gifts have already been placed under the tree in your living room, but you cannot open them until Christmas. The problem is, you have no calendar, therefore no way of knowing beforehand just how long before that day will arrive—or when you will pass over to the other side, which is not something you want to celebrate, at least not since the invention of pain medications, rendering this life much more bearable, if not blessed.

The substance of the gospel focuses not only on this life, but especially on eternal life. Paul told the church at Corinth, "If for this life only we have hoped in Christ, we are of all people most to be pitied" (1 Cor 15:19). He also said, "Beloved . . . this one thing I do: forgetting what lies behind and straining forward to what lies ahead, I press on toward the goal for the prize of the heavenly call of God in Christ Jesus" (Phil 3:13–14).

As you pray this Scripture, imagine what your eternal life now hidden with Christ in God will be like. And through prayer, you can begin to cross over into that life right now. Silently and softly let a bright, warm, and safe cloud enter you as you enter it.

HEBREWS 12:1–3: THE CLOUD OF WITNESSES

WHENEVER YOU PRAY, YOU enter into what has been called "the cloud of God," as God's hidden Spirit silently descends upon you. You enter heaven's eternal time and space, where you may come to know God directly with your spirit, but not with your mind; where you may see God with your heart, but not with your eyes; where you may hear God with your soul, but not with your ears. In that cloud, you also join and are joined by all the generations of Christians who have preceded you in the fulfillment of their faith, and who seek to encourage you to fight the good fight all the way to the end, when you will share with them a destiny in heaven.

This renders prayer all the richer with meaning. Here is the deal: *Prayer and worship are going on in heaven and on earth at one and the same time*, concurrently. That means we are not alone. The souls of dearly departed family members and friends are with us, as we are with them. Our communion with God also includes our communion with them. We may sense, but cannot prove, this great commonality between the living and the dead, but it is there nevertheless. Our common prayer and worship transcend time and space. We are sharing in a unity to be ours forever in heaven.

The writer of Hebrews beautifully describes this extraordinary connection between us and those who have gone before us, who have passed over into heaven and who seek to inspire us from there to join them:

> Therefore, since we are surrounded by so great a cloud of witnesses, let us also lay aside every weight and the sin that clings so closely, and let us run with perseverance the race that is set before us, looking to Jesus the pioneer and perfecter of our faith, who for the sake of the joy that was set before him endured the cross, disregarding its shame, and has taken his seat at the right hand of the throne of God. Consider him who endured such

hostility against himself from sinners, so that you may not grow weary or lose heart. (Heb 12:1–3)

When I pray this Scripture, it always inspires me to continue moving forward with my life and calling from God. I seek to follow those who went before me, and who are there with me now in that cloud invisibly, silently cheering me on. The continuation and consummation of the Christian faith is at stake every time one generation hands it off baton-like to the next generation. With that faith knowledge, we dare not grow weary or lose heart. Pray for the energy and heart of Jesus, of God with us, who is also God in us. He will not rest or grow weary; and in him, neither shall we.

I JOHN 4:7–12, 16–19:
GOD IS LOVE

AMONG THE GREAT TRUTHS we have difficulty taking in and truly believing, is that not only does God love; God *is* Love. No one has ever stated this more clearly than the apostle John:

> Beloved, let us love one another, because love is from God; everyone who loves is born of God and knows God. Whoever does not love does not know God, for God is love. God's love was revealed among us in this way: God sent his only Son into the world so that we might live through him. In this is love, not that we loved God but that he loved us and sent his Son to be the atoning sacrifice for our sins. Beloved, since God loved us so much, we also ought to love one another. No one has ever seen God; if we love one another, God lives in us, and his love is perfected in us . . . .
>
> So we have known and believe the love that God has for us. God is love, and those who abide in love abide in God, and God abides in them. Love has been perfected among us in this: that we may have boldness on the day of judgment, because as he is, so are we in this world. There is no fear in love, but perfect love casts out fear; for fear has to do with punishment, and whoever fears has not reached perfection in love. We love because he first loved us. (1 John 4:7–12, 16–19)

You cannot love and fear at the same time. And God seeks your love above all. To "fear the Lord" means to reverence the God who is love. Who knows but that God secretly comes to us now as love itself. I have written:

O Love, you weary servant in our midst, who hides your crown amidst your concern for us, forgive us for failing to see the holiness of your worker's hands and respond with adequate adoration to the quality of your touch.

We are yet to awaken to your humble ministries, sustaining, nourishing, healing us. We are still too busy taking, to notice the One from whom we take, too focused on the gifts to turn and take in the Giver.

You have ever been our servant, O Love who is God, preferring to wash our feet without words or fanfare, rather than to sit before us on the throne you alone may occupy.

One day you will return to your throne and judge your work.

In prayer, commit yourself to sensing God as the hidden substance of your loving and being loved. That also means God abides *between* you and others as well as *within* you.

REVELATION 3:20: CHRIST IS KNOCKING AT YOUR DOOR

MOST OF US HAVE a problem listening. It seems to be something of a universal issue among humankind. I mean really listening, listening with ear of your heart as well as of your head. We readily take in surface stuff, but to get the fuller, deeper message that might be coming our way, we have to stop what we are doing and truly open up, like flowers in the morning sun. Psalm 46:10 puts this very simply: "Be still, and know that I am God!" You have to be still and silent to take in, learn, and know. And to do that, you really have to want to hear the message.

One of the most remarkable verses in the entire Bible is Revelation 3:20. It presents a great summary of what Christ seeks to do, and for us to do in response, all in Christ's own voice. The resurrected Christ tells the church at Laodicea, "Listen! I am standing at the door, knocking; if you hear my voice and open the door, I will come in to you and eat with you, and you with me" (Rev 3:20). These are words to take to heart and even memorize. I silently recite them nearly every day. It helps keep me opened to, centered, and focused on Christ.

In the Hebrew language of the Old Testament, the word for "listen" is *shema*. The creedal statement of Judaism for thousands of years, to be recited twice a day, is called the *shema*. It comes from Deuteronomy 6:4: "Hear, O Israel: The LORD our God, the LORD is one." Most significantly, that verse is immediately followed by what Jesus called greatest of all God's commandments: "You shall love the LORD your God with all your heart, and with all your soul, and with all your might. Keep these words that I am commanding you today in your heart" (Deut 6:5–6).

Seek to open to and listen for God today. Meditate on this passage from Revelation. Hear these words as if Christ is actually addressing you at the door of your heart. It is for you alone to open that door in the freedom God has granted you. You have to desire and choose to invite God into your heart and soul. If you are truly able to do so, let Christ do the rest. Imagine the communion you two could have together. That sweet communion is the substance of salvation. It will be yours for all eternity, in eternity. Yet if you are ready, you can begin that communion right now.

PRAYING WITH THE SAINTS

"Prayer is the only channel through which God's great graces and favors may flow into the soul; and if this be once closed, I know no other way He can communicate them."

—St. Teresa of Jesus

"Prayer is the place of refuge for every worry, a foundation for cheerfulness, a source of constant happiness, a protection against sadness."

—St. John Chrysostom

"Without prayer we have neither light nor strength to advance in the way which leads to God."

—St. Alphonsus Maria de Liguori

ABOUT PRAYING
WITH THE SAINTS

CHRISTIANITY NEEDS TO BE modeled, in order to continue to exist from one generation to the next. The truth is, our faith is only a single generation from extinction. Likewise, Christian prayer needs to be modeled. Though they are few in number, over the course of two millennia we have been blessed with some great models of what it means to be Christian, and how we are to model or imitate Jesus Christ. That includes how to pray. We call these few "saints." A saint is one who has given their whole life into God's hands to love and serve God and humanity.

Jesus Christ, who is our ultimate model for all things Christian, taught us how to pray his own prayer, which we call the "Lord's Prayer." It reveals the content of what we are to pray for, and Jesus' own heart in praying. Just so, all of the following prayers of specific saints reveal their passion and heart for God.

When we pray the Lord's Prayer, we can get into Christ's own consciousness of what he wants to matter the most for us when we pray. That includes to whom we are to pray. Jesus authorizes us to use the familiar and intimate term for "Father" when addressing the high and holy God of the cosmos. The Aramaic term Jesus authorizes us to say is "*Abba*," which means "Dad." It is in fact the most important word of the entire Lord's Prayer, establishing the personal context for our relationship with God: Dad. Just say "Dad" to God and mean it, and regardless of whether you sense God's presence, as your one and only divine parent, Dad will be there, listening to and loving you.

When Jesus said "Father," he knew the one to whom he was praying. So also did the saints. Their prayers are to the God of their experience, offered in a relationship already established by Christ, which will last forever. I remember the agnostic husband of one of my parishioners several years ago, who after a worship service said, "You know, Hal, when you pray, I think you really know who you are praying to." I do know who I am praying to, but it is a knowledge I can neither prove nor pass on to anybody else. The reality is, everyone must encounter God on their own. This is the same thing as saying every relationship with God is as unique as fingerprints, voices, and snowflakes. Yet at the same time, every relationship will be as common as fingerprints, voices, and snowflakes. Who but God could pull that off?

As you first read, then pray these prayers of the saints, be aware that each of them knew the one to whom they prayed. I hope you will learn more of the "who" of God through their prayers, as well as the "who" of their heart, followed by your own. Pray these prayers, utilizing the same four questions as praying the Scriptures. Do as a novice painter who would copy one or more of the masters. As you pray along with the saints, their verbal brushstrokes will in time guide you to your own brushstroke and way of praying.

AUGUSTINE OF HIPPO: LOVE GOD AND DO AS YOU PLEASE

AUGUSTINE OF HIPPO (354–430) has been called the most significant Christian theologian after the apostle Paul. He famously said, "Love God and do as you please." While that is very freeing, what that really means is this: if you truly love God, you will want to please God. You will not do anything that is displeasing to God. That is of course an extraordinary challenge. For Saint Augustine, however, this was more than a challenge; it was a command. What he said, more as instruction than prayer, can nevertheless be meditated on as foundational to prayer:

> Therefore once for all this short command is given to you: "Love and do what you will." If you keep silent, keep silent by love: if you speak, speak by love; if you correct, correct by love; if you pardon, pardon by love; let love be rooted in you, and from the root nothing but good can grow.

In short, whatever you do, let it be done in the name and spirit of love. That also signifies the Holy Spirit, which is the very love of God. Take to heart what Peter said, "Above all, love each other deeply, because love covers over a multitude of sins" (1 Pet 4:8).

Another major Christian theologian was Bernard of Clairvaux (1090–1153). He wrote a famous treatise titled *On Loving God*. In that treatise, Saint Bernard said that there were four progressive stages to loving God. First was loving yourself for your own sake. Second was loving God, also for your own sake, namely for the possible benefits for you. Third was loving God for God's sake, after you came to know God. And fourth was loving yourself for God's sake. This surprising final stage is reached when you realize that if you do not love yourself, you will neither thrive nor accept God's love for you.

So where are you in these four progressive stages? It is not that one stage is wrong or sinful; rather it is simply where you happen to be. When you encounter God you will discover decisively that God is the most lovable of all persons imaginable; you will love God because God is who God is, rather than merely for what God can do for you. And then, you will want to love and take good care of yourself for the sake of the God who loves you.

PATRICK OF IRELAND:
CHRIST BE MY EVERYTHING

No one understood oneness with Christ better than Patrick of Ireland (388–461). Though surrounded by myths and legends, Saint Patrick was nevertheless a real person, who did incredible works through the power of Jesus Christ. His twin objectives were the glory of God and the salvation of humanity. His zeal for the Lord was matched by his zeal for souls. Bill Bright, the founder of Campus Crusade for Christ, said what we need to evangelize is a love for Jesus Christ, and because of our love for *him*, "a love for *them*," for humanity as a whole.

Patrick truly embraced both forms of love. In his own words: "I was born of a father who was a Decurion [a minor Roman noble], but I sold my nobility, I blush not to state, nor am I sorry. I sold my nobility for the profit of others. In short, I am a slave in Christ to a foreign land on account of the unspeakable glory of the eternal life which is in Christ, our Lord."

There may have already been Christians in Ireland, but Patrick brought Christ to Ireland in a charismatic and permanent fashion. In only thirty years, he transformed a group of Druid tribes into a Christian nation. He himself reportedly founded over three hundred churches, baptized more than one hundred thousand persons, and ordained around five thousand priests and 350 bishops. Patrick became their patron saint. He did so by representing Christ in his own person, and powerfully proclaiming the good news of Jesus Christ. He imprinted the mark of Christ on the Irish people as enduringly as the shamrock, which he apparently used as a symbol for the Trinity, and which Ireland adopted as its own symbol. Truly, Patrick and Ireland are fused together.

Patrick's personal prayer, which was reportedly discovered hidden in his breastplate after his death, could be called the "Christ be my everything" prayer, for its terse petitions contain the essence of the Christian life: a life of mission with, in, and through Jesus Christ. Its power rests in its pure

"Christ-consciousness." It simply asks: "Christ be one with me!" Though there is more than one version available, the following one especially speaks to me.

As you read this prayer, also pray it, getting into its rhythm, and perhaps praying it multiple times:

> Christ be with me, Christ within me,
> Christ behind me, Christ before me,
> Christ beside me, Christ to win me,
> Christ to comfort and restore me,
> Christ beneath me, Christ above me,
> Christ in quiet, Christ in danger,
> Christ in hearts of all that love me,
> Christ in mouth of friend and stranger.

Praying Patrick's prayer can bring you comfort and strength. It can intensify your faith to move forward unafraid; for in truth, Christ is with you.

ANSELM OF CANTERBURY: BELIEF COMES BEFORE UNDERSTANDING

AUGUSTINE OF HIPPO (354–430) famously said: "Understanding is the reward of faith. Therefore, seek not to understand that you may believe, but believe that you may understand." And Anselm of Canterbury (1033–1109) added, "I do not seek to understand so that I can believe, but I believe so that I may understand; and what is more, I believe that unless I do believe, I shall not understand."

It is as if belief opens up an inner treasure trove of understanding impossible to attain without prior faith. The writer of the letter to the Hebrews said, "Now faith is the substance of things hoped for, the evidence of things not seen" (Heb 11:1 NKJV). And the Christian philosopher Soren Kierkegaard (1813–1855) wrote about the necessity of taking a "leap of faith," with understanding coming after the faith-risk of leaping. The amazing truth is that faith is self-authenticating; sufficient proof reveals itself *only after* the risk of believing.

As you meditate on this ancient insight, pray with Saint Anselm his prayer seeking the knowledge of God:

> O my God, teach my heart where and how to seek You, where and how to find You.
>
> You are my God and You are my all and I have never seen You.
>
> You have made me and remade me, You have bestowed on me all the good things I possess,
>
> Still I do not know You.
>
> I have not yet done that for which I was made.
>
> Teach me to seek You.
>
> I cannot seek You unless You teach me or find You unless You show Yourself to me.

Let me seek You in my desire, let me desire You in my seeking.
Let me find You by loving You, let me love You when I find You.
Amen.

While none of us has ever seen God, we are nevertheless capable of sensing God as directly as our skin senses the wind. When you risk believing in God and God's active, actual presence with you, God will, in God's timing and way, authenticate your faith. Guaranteed. In August of 1967, I risked belief in Jesus' words about seeking and finding, risked belief in a yet unknown God. I then began searching, seeking God with my whole heart, as Anselm's prayer so beautifully expresses it. In late November of that year, God's Holy Spirit, the very wind-love of God, breathed upon me, changing my life forever.

Many years later, while praying during a time of troubling doubt, Jesus said to me: "To see me, you must first believe that I am with you. I show myself only to the eyes of faith."

BERNARD OF CLAIRVAUX: THE SWEETNESS OF CHRIST'S LOVE

BERNARD OF CLAIRVAUX (1090–1153) was called "the man of the twelfth century." His vision of the full extent of the Christian's spiritual journey and destiny, together with his grasp of the nature of love, are second to none in church history. His exquisite descriptions of romantic love between God and the soul may well have helped to trigger the entrance into and fixation on romantic love in the Middle Ages, which continues unabated unto the present moment.

It is said that Saint Bernard had a "honey-sweet voice." And he extolled the sweetness of Christ and Christ's love for us. His prayer of praise to Jesus connects divine sweetness with human joy. From the former arises the latter:

> Jesus, how sweet is the very thought of you! You fill my heart with joy. The sweetness of your love surpasses the sweetness of honey. Nothing sweeter than you can be described; no words can express the joy of your love. Only those who have tasted your love for themselves can comprehend it. In your love you listen to all my prayers, even when my wishes are childish, my words confused, and my thoughts foolish. And you answer my prayers, not according to my own misdirected desires, which would only bring bitter misery; but according to my real needs, which brings me sweet joy. Thank you, Jesus, for giving yourself to me.

What effect might the sweetness of Jesus have upon you? As you meditate on this prayer and the sweetness of the love of Christ for you, I will share my own reaction. The love of Jesus being sweet calms me at once, and heightens my confidence to approach him without fear, but rather with open tenderness, to match his own tenderness for me. With sweetness is also understanding and gentleness, and Jesus' gentleness brightens my love for him, as well as my desire to draw near to him. Such silent sweetness includes an acceptance of me as I am, and a responsiveness to my prayers, ever directed at what I really need, rather than what I think I want.

Central to our faith is the actual sense, if not experience, even taste, of Jesus' love for us. As Jesus said, "No one has greater love than this, to lay down one's life for one's friends" (John 15:13). What could be sweeter than such a pure, self-giving love? "O taste and see that the LORD is good; happy are those who take refuge in him" (Ps 8:8).

FRANCIS OF ASSISI: THE WAY OF PEACE

OF ALL THOSE DISCIPLES who came after Jesus, none understood, lived, and made peace better than Francis of Assisi (1181–1226). Born the son of a wealthy merchant in Assisi, Italy, Saint Francis was as a youth a lover of pleasure and sport. He became a soldier, and was captured and imprisoned. While in prison, and weakened by serious illness, Francis's religious conversion began. Once released, and during a worship service, Francis heard the Lord tell him to "rebuild my church." Abandoning his former life, he sought to establish a religious order to evangelize among the poor, to bring the joy and love of the Lord to those who needed it most—to the last, the least, and the lost.

His great prayer is ageless, just like the gospel Francis sought to live all his days. Note: *this man of slight frame and ill health was a layperson*, whose great love for Jesus Christ affected his whole generation, from the pope to the poor. This prayer, surely among the most powerful and poignant of all time, continues to deeply affect all who pray it:

> Lord, make me an instrument of your peace; where there is hatred, let me sow love; where there is injury, pardon; where there is doubt, faith; where there is despair, hope; where there is darkness, light; and where there is sadness, joy.
>
> O Divine Master, grant that I may not so much seek to be consoled as to console: to be understood, as to understand; to be loved, as to love; for it is in giving that we receive, it is in pardoning that we are pardoned, and it is in dying that we are born to eternal life.

This prayer reveals what peacemaking looks like in practice, what its elements are, and what we must do to make it real, to live it fully, both within and without: peace with ourselves, with God, and with others. The prayer begins with our being made instruments of peace. This happens through

God's work in Christ, who has secured our forgiveness, our peace with God through the cross. The way of peace begins with our reception of God's un-conditional offer of forgiveness, life, and love through Christ. *Peace received must become peace acted on, given to others—or it may be lost.*

You can begin the peace process through praying and seeking to live out this prayer. Note: this prayer really has no beginning or ending; rather, its message is self-repeating and timeless. The first stanza brings me to silent stillness every time I hear or read it: "Lord, make me an instrument of your peace." I open afresh to God, and say, "Yes, Lord; please do so."

MECHTHILD OF MAGDEBURG: DANCING WITH GOD

MECHTHILD OF MAGDEBURG (1210–1280), in Northern Germany, was a complicated and profound spiritual writer and nun. And she was something of a free spirit, whose prayers speak to a modern audience. She speaks to me deeply, especially when she connects prayer with dancing. Why not prayer as dancing with God? We get so stiff and formal and burdensome in our praying that we forget that prayer is also to be joyous, even fun. Like the love song says, "Heaven, I'm in heaven . . . when we're out together, dancing cheek to cheek." Let your heart dance with Mechthild in her prayer:

> I cannot dance, O Lord, unless you lead me. If it is your will, I can leap with joy. But you must show me how to dance and sing by dancing and singing yourself! With you I will leap towards love, and from love I will leap to truth, and from truth I will leap to joy, and then I shall leap beyond all human senses. There I will remain and dance for evermore.

Though your body may not dance while in prayer, your spirit can. You can move with the Holy Spirit, who is ever in motion, like the wind. As Jesus said, "The wind blows where it chooses, and you hear the sound of it, but you do not know where it comes from or where it goes. So it is with everyone who is born of the Spirit" (John 3:8).

I have moved with the Spirit-wind and danced with God in prayer. I wrote to God:

Thank you for moving toward me silently, graciously across the darkened dance floor with markers but no beginning or end;

Thank you for reaching out with assured, assuring hands inviting me to join you in a dance unfamiliar yet strangely that for which I seem gladly made.

Thank you for leading me around and around the clouded floor liltingly, laughingly, lovingly, longingly;

Thank you for guiding me through a dance of your design alone, yet whose rhythms arise in my heart in harmonic response to your turning me this way and that in an embrace that will not end as long as I am;

For I will cleave to you in heart and spirit, should you move on to other partners and dances beyond my vision.

You may well dance with God in heaven. Begin now by letting God lead you in prayer.

CATHERINE OF SIENA: MY NATURE IS FIRE

CATHERINE OF SIENA (1347–1380) was one of the greatest mystic-saints of all time. In her short life, she had a profound impact on the church. You could say that she was "on fire" for Christ. She had a charismatic personality, and could persuade others to see things her way. Catherine's book *The Dialogue* was the second book published by the first printing press, after the Gutenberg Bible. She would become one of the thirty-three "Doctors" of the Catholic Church, the second woman to be so honored.

In 1366 while in her room, Saint Catherine had a vision of a mystical marriage with Jesus, and would subsequently claim to have experienced a heart exchange with the Christ's heart. After this miraculous exchange, she told her confessor Fra Tommaso, "Can't you see, Father, that I am not the person I was, but am changed into someone else?" And she went on, "My mind is so full of joy and happiness that I am amazed my soul stays in my body." She also said, "There is so much heat in my soul that this material fire seems cool by comparison, rather than to be giving out heat; it seems to have gone out, rather than to be still burning."

In her bold prayer, Catherine said her nature, like that of God, was fire. I myself have experienced the fire of Christ's heart in my own heart. Be open to Christ's heart if and as you are willing to pray Catherine's prayer:

> In your nature, eternal Godhead, I shall come to know my nature. And what is my nature, boundless love? It is fire, because you are nothing but a fire of love. And you have given humankind a share in this nature, for by the fire of love you created us. And so with all other people and every created thing; you made them out of love. O ungrateful people! What nature has your God given you? His very own nature! Are you not ashamed to cut yourself off from such a noble thing through the guilt of deadly sin? O eternal Trinity, my sweet love! You, light, give

us light. You, wisdom, give us wisdom. You, supreme strength, strengthen us. Today, eternal God, let our cloud be dissipated so that we may perfectly know and follow your Truth in truth, with a free and simple heart. God, come to our assistance! Lord, make haste to help us!

As you pray this prayer, if you are ready, ask the Lord to warm your heart. John Wesley had his heart "strangely warmed," in 1835, and he subsequently led a great revival in England which gave rise to the "people called 'Methodists.'"

MECHTHILD OF HACKEBORN: LET CHRIST BE EVERYWHERE

ONE OF THE EXTRAORDINARY mystics and lovers of Christ was Mechthild of Hackeborn (1241–1298). She reported amazing dialogues with Christ, as recorded in her *The Book of Special Grace*. Saint Mechthild herself did not write the work; rather two other mystic nuns wrote down her experiences, as Christ commanded them to do. Once, after Mechthild expressed her fervent desire to be in perpetual union with Christ, the Lord said to her:

> Above you I will be hope and joy to uplift you. Within you I will be life-giving life and gladdening food, richly feasting your soul. Behind you I will be desire propelling you forward; before you I will be love, alluring and caressing your soul. At your right hand I will be praise, perfecting all your works; at your left hand, a golden couch supporting you in trials; beneath you a firmament sustaining your soul.

These words are reminiscent of the prayer of St. Patrick, found in his breastplate, and which we explored earlier. Patrick reportedly wrote it for divine protection in 433, as he sought to convert Ireland to Christ. It expressed how everywhere he hoped Christ would be for him (e.g., above me, below me, within me, behind me, before me). It turned out that both Patrick and Mechthild were quite successful in their endeavors for Christ.

The major difference between the two statements about Christ being present everywhere is that Patrick wrote his prayer, whereas Mechthild heard Christ say this to her, as a vow of protective presence throughout her life. What Christ said to her should be taken into the hearts and hopes of all Christians, for all time. Christ said, in effect, "Do not fear for your life in any way, anywhere, during any day, for I will ever be with you: above, within, behind, before, at your right and left, and beneath you, as your rock upon which to build your home in this world."

What would your daily life be like if Christ said these things to you? Once in a dream, God said to me, "Do not fear another day in your life!" Henceforth, should I fear (though I have), that would constitute a failure to thrive in spite of God's gracious presence with me.

Seek to live out of these words: "The LORD is my light and my salvation; whom shall I fear? The LORD is the stronghold of my life; of whom shall I be afraid?" (Ps 27:1).

GERTRUDE OF HELFTA: MAY YOUR WORK UNITE WITH CHRIST'S WORK

GERTRUDE OF HELFTA (1256–1302) did not like to talk about herself, except to say how unworthy she was of the graces God bestowed upon her. Her experiences of God were such that the epithet "the Great" would later be added to her name. Saint Gertrude entered the monastery school at Helfta, Germany, at the young age of four, and her encounters with Jesus and his heart were astounding, as was her book, which Christ himself assigned her to write, including its title: *The Herald of Divine Love.*

Gertrude was something of a free spirit. In fact, during a prayer Mechthild of Hackeborn asked Christ, "Why it was that, although she has lived so long in the presence of God, Gertrude seems to be living in such a negligent way?" The Lord reportedly answered: "*Her freedom of heart.* . . . I have always found her ready to receive my gifts, for she permits nothing to remain in her heart which might impede my action."

I, too, seek to always be ready to receive Christ's gifts, and to permit nothing to remain in my heart which might impede God's action. Quite the opposite. I seek that whatever I do is of God, by God, and for God. This prayer of Gertrude is also the prayer of my heart:

> Lord, in union with your love, unite my work with your great work, and perfect it. As a drop of water poured into a river is taken up into the activity of the river, so may my labor become part of your work. May those among whom I live and work be drawn into your love.

Once during a prayer long ago, I had an unmistakable sense of my will uniting with God's will. It was as in my human will was poured into the infinite river of God's will. At once in God's current, we were moving in the same direction at the same speed. And the comforting sense, so clear and intense, was that what I wanted, God also wanted, and vice versa. At that moment I asked God to keep my will in God's will, for I want nothing more in life than to do God's will. And to have whatever work I do be united with the work of God.

When I do pass over, I want above all to hear the words, "Well done, good and trustworthy servant." I can think of no greater honor.

IGNATIUS OF LOYOLA: OVERCOMING DEPRESSION

IGNATIUS OF LOYOLA (1491–1556) was not only a priest, but also a soldier for Jesus Christ and his church. He cofounded the religious order called the Society of Jesus (Jesuits) in 1540. He also authored the *Spiritual Exercises*, a set of prayers and meditations and simple exercises. Saint Ignatius was not unfamiliar with the vulnerabilities of religious life, including depression and darkness. Depression has a spirituality as well as a biology and psychology. And in his prayer, facing darkness unafraid, Ignatius recognizes and calls upon the power of Jesus Christ to heal and strengthen his body and soul. Truly, no one can heal the soul as well as the Lord and his love. In cleaving to Christ in spirit, Christ will dispel our darkness and doubts. Thus did Ignatius pray:

> O Christ Jesus, when all is darkness and we feel our weakness and helplessness, give us the sense of Your presence, Your love, and Your strength.
>
> Help us to have perfect trust in Your protecting love and strengthening power, so that nothing may frighten or worry us, for, living close to You, we shall see Your hand, Your purpose, Your will through all things.

When, not if, we go through periods of darkness, doubt, and depression, this prayer addresses Christ with a simple plea for assistance. In a word, that is what Ignatius is praying for, and that is really all we need to ask for: *Help.* And when help comes, all we really need to say to God is a two-word prayer. As long as it is heartfelt like the first prayer, simply say: *Thank you.*

And when God moves us through and out of depression, Ignatius offers us yet another prayer to bolster our passion for God and to solidify our purpose for living. It is a call to action:

Dearest Lord, teach me to be generous; teach me to serve You as You deserve; to give and not to count the cost, to fight and not to heed the wounds, to toil and not to seek for rest, to labor and not to ask for reward save that of knowing I am doing Your Will.

This second prayer always stirs in me greater strength and commitment to serve God. It is a prayer to memorize and recite daily, especially before facing any challenge or difficulty. Like putting on the whole armor of God (Eph 6:10–18), this prayer prepares us to do something for the Lord.

TERESA OF AVILA: ON FAITH AND FEARLESSNESS

THE PRAYER OF TERESA of Avila (1515–82), which was found in her breviary after her death, has inspired me and countless others. Saint Teresa was a Spanish Carmelite nun, whose spiritual depth and mystical writing led to her becoming one of the thirty-three "Doctors of the Church." Though brief, its impact can be profound. Let these words lead you to more confident prayer. What do they say to you? What do you want to say to God? What does God want to say to you?

> Let nothing disturb you,
> Let nothing frighten you,
> All things are passing away:
> God never changes.
> Patient endurance attains all things
> Whoever has God lacks nothing;
> God alone suffices.
> [or "If you have only God, you have more than enough"].

Let us briefly examine each verse:

"Let nothing disturb you." This is doable only when you commit yourself into God's hands, and risk trusting that no evil will befall you—except that which God permits, for your maturing and eternal well-being.

"Let nothing frighten you." If God is for you, who can be against you? As the psalmist said: "The LORD is my light and my salvation; whom shall I fear? The LORD is the stronghold of my life; of whom shall I be afraid?" (Ps 27:1).

"All things are passing away." A wise woman once told me, while I was in the midst of a crisis: "This, too, will pass." Her words proved true, and I have repeated it to numerous others.

"God never changes." God is "the same yesterday, today and forever" (Heb 13:8). The cosmos will come and go, but not its Creator. God is our one unshakable anchor.

"Patient endurance attains all things." Jesus tells us that "By your endurance you will gain your souls" (Luke 21:19). Paul says, "Rejoice in hope, be patient in suffering, persevere in prayer" (Rom 12:12). And James says to "let endurance have its full effect, so that you may be mature and complete, lacking in nothing" (Jas 1:4).

"Whoever has God lacks nothing." With Jesus Christ as our Good Shepherd, you shall not want (Ps 23:1).

"God alone suffices." As a woman who lost her hundred-year family farm once told me, during the farm crisis in the 1980s, adding that these words kept her alive and moving forward: "When you lose everything but God, you will realize that God is all you really need." As the psalmist said: "Whom have I in heaven but you? And there is nothing on earth that I desire other than you" (Ps 73:25).

FRANCIS DE SALES: COMMITMENT TO GOD

OUR FAITH AND COMMITMENT to God must be as unconditional as God's faithfulness and love for us. Francis De Sales (1567–1622) evidenced such faith and commitment to God. A Bishop of Geneva, Italy, he wrote the perennial classic *Introduction to the Devout Life*, and *Treatise on the Love of God*. Saint Francis was a spellbinding preacher, whose motto was, "He who preaches with love, preaches effectively."

Francis's prayer attests to his total devotion to "love eternal":

> O love eternal, my soul needs and chooses you eternally! Ah, come Holy Spirit, and inflame our hearts with your love! To love—or to die! To die—and to love! To die to all other love in order to live in Jesus' love, so that we may not die eternally. But that we may live in your eternal love, O Savior of our souls, we eternally sing, "Live, Jesus! Jesus, I love! Live, Jesus, whom I love! Jesus, I love, Jesus who lives and reigns forever and ever." Amen.

I, too, seek to be totally faithful and committed to God. This is my prayer of commitment. I hope it speaks to you:

My heart is steadfast, O God. I have not moved from you, from the beginning of us. I thrive and will thrive treelike in the garden of our mutual life, where it pleased you to plant me. That is my faith.

My heart is steadfast, O God. Every day I stand at the door of your presence waiting for you. I wait for you as lovers await one another, yearning for your face, your touch, your words, your way, your will. That is my faith.

My heart is steadfast, O God. I wrestle with your remembered Spirit close by and have not let you go, will not let you go until you bless me. The blessing I seek is the constancy of your presence with me, love's unbroken mutual life. That is my faith.

My heart is steadfast, O God. I will endure what I must, but you will find me at the ready to answer your call with, "Here I am!," whenever you choose to call. However long it takes, however much testing I must undergo, I will not turn or close off from you. That is my faith.

My heart is steadfast, O God. That which you began in me, with me, will not end until it ends in you. Your power in me will not be expended until I am safely in an eternal orbit around you, a smiling moon ever facing you, my precious Earth. That is my faith.

BROTHER LAWRENCE: PRACTICING THE PRESENCE OF GOD

SOMETIMES THE SIMPLEST THINGS can be the most profound. That is definitely the case with the book *The Practice of the Presence of God*. It was posthumously compiled from letters and discussions with peers of a humble and unassuming lay brother in a Carmelite monastery in Paris. A disenchanted a young soldier, Nicholas Herman (1614–1691), joined the monastery and took the name Brother Lawrence of the Resurrection. There, he spent the remainder of his life working in the kitchen and repairing his brothers' sandals.

What Brother Lawrence discovered was how to practice the presence of God, no matter where you are or what you are doing. He said he felt closer to God while mopping the kitchen floor than most anywhere else. Today we would probably call this "God-consciousness" or "mindfulness." In the words of Brother Lawrence:

> There is not in the world a kind of life more sweet and delightful, than that of a continual conversation with God; those only can comprehend it who practice and experience it.
>
> The most holy and necessary practice in our spiritual life is the presence of God. That means finding constant pleasure in His divine company, speaking humbly and lovingly with him in all seasons, at every moment, without limiting the conversation in any way.
>
> I have abandoned all particular forms of devotion, all prayer techniques. My only prayer practice is attention. I carry on a habitual, silent, and secret conversation with God that fills me with overwhelming joy.

How do you do this? Simply begin by imagining and acting *as if* God is right there with you, at that very moment and always. Then carry on telepathic conversations with God. At some point, and this I guarantee, you will actually sense God's presence, even participation. Then you will realize that God has truly been with you all the while.

I discovered this years ago, after praying with a dying man and seeking to comfort his family. Right after that, I had to go and take out the garbage at our family's Green's Tea and Coffee Shop. Here I was, lifting two heavy garbage containers, and carrying them downstairs to the dumpster. From a poignant end-of-life-prayer, to dumping garbage. Just minutes apart. Then I thought of Brother Lawrence, and determined to practice the "presence of God," on the spot. Sure enough, I came to sense God's presence, even emptying garbage. The ancients were right: *"God is wherever you let God in."*

MARGARET MARY ALACOQUE: LOVE OF THE SACRED HEART

MARGARET MARY ALACOQUE (1647–1690) is the person whom the Lord commanded to establish the "Devotion to the Sacred Heart of Jesus Christ" tradition. Saint Margaret, a member of the Sisters of the Visitation in France, had dramatic encounters with Jesus, including an exchanging of hearts. Here is part of her first "great revelation" concerning the Sacred Heart:

> Once when I was before the blessed sacrament . . . I was suddenly completely surrounded by the divine presence. It was so intense I lost my sense of who and where I was. I abandoned myself to the Spirit, yielding my heart to the power of his love. He made me rest for a long time on his divine breast where he showed me the marvels of his love and the unspeakable secrets of his sacred heart that had always been hidden before. He opened them to me there for the first time, in such a real and tangible way. Even though I am always afraid of deceiving myself about what I say happens inside me, I could not doubt what was happening because of the effects that the grace produced in me.

Her prayer to the Sacred Heart is in loving response to Christ's fathomless love:

> O most amiable Heart, Thou art my strength, my support, my recompense, my safety, my refuge, my love and my all. O most holy Heart of Jesus, Heart most august, Master of all hearts, I love Thee, I adore Thee, I praise Thee; I thank Thee, I wish to be all Thine. O Heart of love, dwell with me and in me; govern me, save me, change me entirely into Thee. O most excellent and most Sacred Heart, the eternal enjoyment of which will be, without surfeit, the Source of enjoyment and the Recompense

of the blessed, how desirable, how lovable Thou art! O Divine Heart, come to me or draw me to Thee. O Heart most sublime, the Delight of Divinity! I salute Thee from exile where I am; I invoke Thee in my sorrow; I call on Thee as the remedy for my frailty. Oh! most merciful Heart, compassionate and generous Heart of my Father and my Savior, do not refuse Thy help to my unworthy heart . . . that Thy image may be completely perfected in me and that it may one day be an ornament in Thy Heavenly palace. Amen.

Let your heart appeal to the heart of Jesus. Heart-to-heart messages are most effective.

JOHN WESLEY: LET GO AND LET GOD

A PRAYER OF TOTAL self-giving by John Wesley (1703–1791), who founded the Methodist Church, has been my constant companion for decades. It is about letting go of control, and letting God be in charge, something very difficult for me and for most all of us:

> I am no longer my own but Yours,
> Put me to what You will,
> Put me to doing. Put me to suffering,
> Let me be employed for You, or laid aside for You,
> Exulted for You, or brought low for You.
> Let me be full, let me be empty.
> Let me have all things, let me have nothing.
> I freely and wholeheartedly yield all things to
> Your pleasure and disposal.
> And now glorious and blessed God,
> Father, Son and Holy Spirit,
> You are mine and I am Yours, so be it.
> And this covenant now made on earth,
> Let it be satisfied in Heaven.
> Amen.

True religion begins when you realize that you are absolutely dependent upon God. It is when you grasp at your deepest level that you are not the "captain of your soul," as the poem "Invictus," by William Ernest Henley, put it. That poem was close to my mother's heart, and she repeated it with defiant regularity.

When I became a pastor, I adopted Wesley's words, rather than Henley's. I would silently repeat during prayer, "I am no longer my own but

Yours, / Put me to what You will." This was especially problematic to pray during troubling times when I thought I could perhaps do a better job of directing my life than God seemed to be doing.

I remember what a very wise Christian woman told me many years ago. She said that spiritual maturity is attained when you are equally willing to sit on the sidelines or to be on the playing field. As a former football player, I could not imagine ever being equally willing to be held back as a reserve as opposed to being out there on the field, blocking or tackling somebody. At the same time, I sensed she was right, and that I was far from maturity.

Well, I think I have finally reached the point where I am equally willing to do or not to do in accordance with God's will. *Equally willing*, just as long as it is God's will for me. I challenge you to pray Wesley's prayer daily for one week. See what God might have in store for you.

JOHN VIANNEY: LOVING GOD ALL THE WAY

To KNOW GOD IS to love God. As God draws near, your heart, seemingly of itself, arises with love unspeakable. You do not have to think or decide to love God; God is love itself. Hence, the love arising in you as God becomes present to you, is also God arising in you.

French priest Saint John Vianney (1786–1859) understood this equation between God and love. For him, the meaning of life was to love God above all, in all and through all. His prayer is beautiful and brings beauty to the soul of the person who prays it:

> I love You, O my God, and my only desire is to love You until the last breath of my life. I love You, O my infinitely lovable God, and I would rather die loving You, than live without loving You. I love You, Lord, and the only grace I ask is to love You eternally . . . My God, if my tongue cannot say in every moment that I love You, I want my heart to repeat it to You as often as I draw breath.

More than love, I am in love with the God I have encountered. Thus I have prayed:

May I not speak of you save with words of love. You are not an object for casual discussion; you are the daily Subject of my life.

May I not speak of you with anything but love's tones and timbres, toward any end but love's.

More than love you . . . I remain irrevocably in love with you, the God of all creation. Yet who am I to dare to make such a claim, to be in love with you, in love as a tree with the sky toward which it reaches, or a river with the sea toward which it flows?

Did you not know my heart would follow after you in spirit if not in body once I met you? Did you not know I would want nothing more than to live with you in this love, than to share a common life with you? Did you not know you would become my furthest aim and Beloved above all else?

I speak to you with words of love because they are the only words worthy of you, the only words which may attain an audience with you.

Heaven is the home of those in love with you. Heaven is the home of those who will not speak of you save with words of love.

Pray this prayer, and ask that the love of God *for* you, once received, may then become the love of God, *from* you. Then God's holy circle of love will be complete, love from God returning to God as love for God from you.

KAHLIL GIBRAN: A
PRAYER TO LOVE

KAHLIL GIBRAN (1883–1931), WHO wrote the masterpiece *The Prophet*, also wrote a prayer poem titled, simply, "Love," which spoke to my heart more than five decades ago. I discovered it shortly after I first encountered God and within a week met the woman who would become the love of my life. Prior to these two yoked events, I had been an agnostic "man of the world," having been in relationships with other women. Now I sought in earnest to clean up my life in every sense, so as to become a better man, and above all to remain true to love and fidelity for the remainder of my life.

Gibran's prayer poem gave me the words I could and did commit myself to carrying out, day in and day out. I also vowed never to sacrifice a greater value for a lesser one. While I have had my temptations, my trials and tribulations, I have nevertheless continued to honor God, love, and my beloved wife.

Gibran's prayer poem to love, and to the God who is love, addresses the true power and goodness of love, together with the vowed commitment of one who has finally found true love to faithfully serve it. I have returned to this prayer at least yearly, to recommit myself to love, as to God:

> They say the jackal and the mole
> Drink from the self-same stream
> Where the lion comes to drink.
>
> And they say the eagle and the vulture
> Dig their beaks into the same carcass,
> And are at peace, one with the other
> In the presence of the dead thing.

O Love, whose lordly hand
Has bridled my desires,
And raised my hunger and thirst
To dignity and pride,
Let not the strong in me and the constant
Eat the bread or drink the wine
That tempt my weaker self.
Let me rather starve,
And let my heart parch with thirst,
And let me die and perish,
Ere I stretch my hand
To a cup you did not fill,
Or a bowl you did not bless.

If to nothing or no one else, commit yourself to be true to the God who is love. That may require some self-forgiveness, as well as the forgiveness of others. But let nothing or no one stop you from the profound commitment voiced in Gibran's prayer. For me, the heart of this commitment, is "Ere I stretch my hand / To a cup you did not fill, / Or a bowl you did not bless."

MOTHER TERESA: THE FRUIT OF PRAYER

MOTHER TERESA OF CALCUTTA (1910–1997) was one of the true models of the love of Jesus Christ for all humanity. A tireless worker for the destitute in poverty-stricken Calcutta, India, she responded wholeheartedly to Jesus' call for her to "bring my love to the poorest of the poor." Saint Mother Teresa founded the Sisters of Charity, and worked with the multitude of homeless, especially those left to die on the streets of Calcutta. She sought to get them off the streets, to comfort and restore their sense of dignity. She wanted them to know that they, too, were loved children of God.

One of Mother Teresa's profound insights about prayer is worthy of meditation and application to our own lives. This should be prayed as well as read through. The words may be few, but their impact can be profound:

> The fruit of silence is prayer,
> the fruit of prayer is faith,
> the fruit of faith is love,
> the fruit of love is service,
> and the fruit of service is peace.

A few comments on this extraordinary prayer statement:

"*The fruit of silence is prayer.*" Prayer leads to and blossoms in silence. In God-assisted silence, what seeks expression within you, as well as what God seeks to say or show you, may finally be sensed, if not heard by the ear of your heart. Remember that God summons you to "Be still, and know that I am God!" (Ps 46:10). Hence, if you ask God to help you attain silent stillness, and are thereby enabled to become God-conscious rather than self-conscious, God-assisted silence will follow as a gift of grace.

"*The fruit of prayer is faith.*" Faith is both one of the gifts and also one of the fruit of the Holy Spirit. Faith arises and increases as you open to God in prayer. The truth is, "Little prayer, little faith; much prayer, much faith."

"The fruit of faith is love." Without faith, who among us is willing to open our hearts and risk loving and being loved? Faith constitutes the very ground of love.

"The fruit of love is service." Once love has risen like a spring flowing from a heart steeped in prayer and built up in faith, love seeks to be of service. As Kahlil Gibran said, "Work is love made visible."

"The fruit of service is peace." There is a kind of grateful peace which emerges when you have actively sought to make a difference in the lives of others. As Mother Teresa had it, rather than seeking to do great things with little love, you should seek to do little things with great love.

HENRI NOUWEN: TURN CONTROL OVER TO GOD

HENRI NOUWEN (1932–1996) WAS a Dutch Catholic priest, a professor and writer, a theologian, psychologist, and spiritual mentor to many, myself included. He was a loving and gentle soul, who in his final years worked with individuals with intellectual and developmental disabilities at the L'Arche Daybreak community in Richmond Hill, Ontario. His prayer:

> Dear God, I so much want to be in control. I want to be the master of my own destiny. Still I know that you are saying: "Let me take you by the hand and lead you. Accept my love and trust that where I will bring you, the deepest desires of your heart will be fulfilled." Lord, open my hands to receive your gift of love. Amen.

This prayer of Fr. Nouwen aims directly at something most all of us struggle with throughout our lives: turning control of our lives over to God. We want to be in control; we secretly want the power to be as our own God, even for the best of reasons, to give to rather than take from humanity. We want to be in charge of our daily existence, so we can "seize the day" (*carpe diem*). That includes securing the well-being of ourselves and our loved ones.

As I have noted, one of my mother's favorite poems was "Invictus," by William Ernest Henley. She knew it by heart and would quote it to me in effort to inspire me to take control over my life and do great things. In part, Henley wrote: "Out of the night that covers me, / Black as the pit from pole to pole, / I thank whatever gods may be / For my unconquerable soul . . . / It matters not how strait the gate, / How charged with punishments the scroll, / I am the master of my fate, / I am the captain of my soul."

That may sound good until life throws you some painful obstacles, and you realize that without divine assistance you may not make it through the difficulty. Such obstacles can prove to be for your ultimate benefit, prompting you to turn to God, who has been with you all along, waiting for you. During one such a time in my life, when I thought I might not make it, I prayed to God daily for months this prayer of relinquishment: "I am in your Hands, Lord. I exist because of you, and for you. Do with me as you will." Fortunately, it was God's will to see me through my difficulty. In my absolute dependence on God, God drew me nearer than ever before. Strange how connected such radical reliance on God is to the freedom to be fearlessly who I really am.

Giving control of your life over to God is something you have to do daily. The inviolate truth is, God knows best and will do what is best for you, not just for now, but for eternity.

MEDITATIVE PRAYER

"Finally, beloved, whatever is true, whatever is honorable, whatever is just, whatever is pure, whatever is pleasing, whatever is commendable, if there is any excellence and if there is anything worthy of praise, think about these things."

(PHIL 4:8).

"I just have to do prayers and meditation and affirmations to myself as I go throughout the day, and that's the only way I'm able to make it through some days."

—VALERIE JUNE

"Though my needs may drive me to prayer, it is there I come face to face with my greatest need: an encounter with God Himself."

—PHILIP YANCEY

ABOUT MEDITATIVE PRAYER

MEDITATIVE PRAYER FOLLOWS THE same four steps as praying the Scriptures (*Lectio Divina*). That is, reading, meditation, prayer, and contemplation, leading to four questions:

1. What does the text say?
2. What does it say to me?
3. What do I want to say to God?
4. What does God want to say to me?

To meditate means to ruminate about, ponder, reflect on the possible significance of a prayer to you. First you read the meditation in its entirety. Then you follow where your heart and eyes take you. Whatever it is, from a single word to an entire stanza, what is it saying to you? This puts you into a dialogue with the passage, asking questions and listening to what the text might be saying to you, and perhaps what God might be saying to you through the text.

At some point, you will find yourself wanting to include God in the dialogue between you and the text. This then becomes a dialogical prayer, with God on one end and you on the other, with the text between the two of you.

Finally, whether during your meditative prayer or after, you will hopefully sense a divine response of some sort. It could involve a shift to a better mood, since God can affect your emotions directly. It could be any of the means described above in the section "How God Speaks to Us in Prayer." God usually prefers the soft approach of understating, so as to not generate fear on your part. I have heard fascinating stories of God messages, from persons who were uncomfortable telling their stories due to possible adverse reactions.

To begin meditative prayer, I offer one of my meditations, titled "Restoration." It addresses a time of doubt in God, and God's restoration of my all-important faith.

You restored my faith.

Faith seemed to have left me; I found myself floating listless on the doldrums of doubt.

I had some time back turned off course, so slightly at first it passed by my notice.

Then doubt's foggy fingers stealthily engulfed my vessel.

Darkening gray closed over everything; losing sight of the sky, I could not determine my whereabouts, or what heading to take.

Night set in, and the wind died down to death.

I stayed afloat on hope's good promise of warm winds with the return of day.

Yet even before daylight, in the darkest beating of the night, you brought me a bright breeze, restoring my faith, filling my sails with a shout.

Gladly I let your winds set my course.

Following where you led me, I emerged from the flattening fog onto the dawning blue sea wed to the lightening blue sky.

I met afresh your trade winds, your chosen currents for faith's sure journey unto you.

O LOVE THAT WILL
NOT LET ME GO

SOMETIMES A HYMN CAN speak to you, almost as if from heaven. Such a hymn is "O Love That Wilt Not Let Me Go." It has haunted yet calmed me over the years. I even wrote music for it. It is inspired and worthy to gently meditate:

> Oh Love, that wilt not let me go,
> I rest my weary soul in Thee;
> I give Thee back the life I owe,
> That in Thine ocean depths its flow
> May richer, fuller be.

> Oh Light, that followest all my way,
> I yield my flickering torch to Thee;
> My heart restores its borrowed ray,
> That in Thy sunshine's blaze its day
> May brighter, fairer be.

> O Joy, that seekest me through pain,
> I cannot close my heart to Thee;
> I trace the rainbow through the rain,
> And feel the promise is not vain
> That morn shall tearless be.

> O Cross, that liftest up my head,
> I dare not ask to fly from Thee;
> I lay in dust's life glory dead,
> And from the ground there blossoms red

Life that shall endless be.

George Matheson (1842–1906) suffered poor eyesight from birth, and at age fifteen learned he was going blind. Not easily discouraged, he enrolled in the University of Glasgow and graduated at age nineteen. He then began theological studies, during which he became totally blind.

On the day that one of his sisters was married, Matheson wrote this hymn. He recorded this account of that experience in his journal:

> My hymn was composed . . . on the evening of June 6, 1882. I was at that time alone. It was the day of my sister's marriage . . . Something had happened to me which was known only to myself, and which caused me the most severe mental suffering. The hymn was the fruit of that suffering. It was the quickest bit of work I ever did in my life. I had the impression of having it dictated to me by some inward voice then of working it out myself. I am quite sure that the whole work was completed in five minutes, and equally sure that it never received at my hands any retouching or correction. I have no natural gift of rhythm. All the other verses I have written are manufactured articles; this came like a dayspring from on high. I have never been able to gain once more the same fervor in verse.

"Oh Love, that wilt not let me go, I rest my weary soul in Thee." Let these humble words of quiet surrender to the ever-present, ever-faithful love of God work their wonder in your heart.

RESTING PRAYER

WE REST BETTER WITH a trusted other, than all alone. Alone, our mind easily wanders to the troubling areas of our life. And before we know it, our inner worrier kicks in, like an intensifying generator with seemingly endless fuel. Yet when we rest with a trusted other, it becomes easier to find peace in that shared moment, to let go of concerns, and to come fully into the present unencumbered by the harassing "what if's" and "could be's" of lonely, all-alone life.

Right after creating the cosmos, God rested. Calling everything God made "good," God entered the first Sabbath (Gen 2:1–3), making it holy. God subsequently commanded humanity to do likewise: work six days a week and then rest on the seventh. God may still be in a Sabbath mode, at least until God creates "a new heaven and a new earth" (Rev 21:1–2).

Resting seems simple and attainable. Yet most of us do not know how to truly rest. We bring our work issues home, and our home issues to work. We need to learn how to let go and let be, to simply rest—and not just when we fall asleep, but also when we are awake.

One thing that works for me I call "resting prayer," where I ask nothing of God, and God asks nothing of me. We simply rest together, silently letting love flow freely between us. And the amazing thing is, this also works well while praying with your dog at your feet, or your cat curled on your lap. I wrote this meditation to God while my dog, Wally, rested at my feet:

I rest upon you, as you rest in me.

We repose together, in wordless wonder, sharing in your Sabbath gift, albeit in different ways as different beings, you as God and me as human.

No work is done; love simply unmasks its silent presence between us.

I offer you these words of thanksgiving, as my shepherd dog rests at my feet, curled between and snuggling them.

He lightly sleeps as I intently pray; yet we are at rest together, different beings united in hushed peace, one wordlessly comforting the other.

Somehow our being together, you and I, Beloved, as well as my dog and I, my well-loved Wally, makes possible this rest.

It turns out I cannot truly rest alone, but only with you; and strangely, sometimes also with my dog, a real instigator of Sabbath moments.

JUST TALK TO GOD

THERE IS NO MYSTERY greater than that of God. God will forever remain a mystery, as you will discover when you encounter God. God will be perpetually surrounded by mystery, rather like the earth being surrounded by its atmosphere. The atmosphere of the earth does not prevent us from flying out of as well as back into it. It just means that when we return to earth, we must respect its atmosphere and slow down to safely reenter it. So it is also with the everlasting mystery of God: respect the sovereignty of God and slow down to utter awe as you draw near to the holy One. Most importantly, once you have entered into and breathed in God's mystical atmosphere, you will never forget its indescribable union of goodness, beauty, and truth. You will simply desire to remain there forever. This I know because, through God's grace, I have flown in prayer into God's mystical atmosphere, which has also been called the "Cloud of Unknowing."

Encountering God will not remove the mystery of God; rather it will purify and even intensify that mystery. You will both know and not know God at the same time, just as you may know the "you" of another person, but not their "I." So it is also with God—but much greater, for the "I" of God is far beyond the limited, limiting "I" of our humanity.

Nevertheless, just talk to God when you pray, without attempting to figure out the who or why of God. Take on faith that God hears you and knows you as none other ever has or shall. And trust that even with such complete knowledge, God continues to love you as none other ever shall. Then let your heart open to God's loving mystery. You will at some point encounter God's endless love within that shrouded mystery of meeting. Embrace and enjoy such rare moments, along with the vivid sense that God has been and will always be with you.

Here is what I said to God in one of my meditative prayers. I invite you to enter into it:

I would rather talk to you than about you.
When I talk about you to others, you are a silent partner in the discussion.

When I talk about you I cannot be who I am with you; I am not in our safe harbor of mutuality, but on the sea of human discourse, where I must beware the shoals of shallow representation and the storms of fretful misunderstanding.

When I talk to you, I become myself as I lose myself in you.

I reenter the harbor of our common life, where the water is always calm and calming, as I slow down to let the lapping water love the vessel of my soul on its way to your shore.

Truly, the living water of the Spirit between God and you will be forever calm and calming, safe and saving.

PRAYER'S MAGIC CARPET

As a child, I used to dream of flying on a magic carpet. Little did I understand back then that prayer can actually become like a magic carpet, first elevating us and then somehow carrying us to God. And just as amazing as flight to God, as subtle motion of prayer, is the equally amazing sense that we have not really moved at all, that we have strangely arrived at where we already were, but did not know it.

Prayer will slowly reveal to us our unique, private yet shared space with God, already in place from the moment of our birth. It is as if God planned out our entire future, our coming time to be alone with God, at the very instant of our creation. How God can wrap our furthest tomorrow right into our initial beginning is an unfathomable mystery. But then, so is God, and likely will forever remain so.

I offer this meditation, summarizing in briefest terms my progressive prayer history with God. You will note that what began as a seemingly small slice of space evolved into an immeasurable expanse, since wherever God is, there also is infinity, in every sense.

Prayer is as an unseen carpet, though not at its beginning, but only as you stay on it, persevering through its moods and colorations.

At first prayer may seem like a narrow patch of grass on which to merely sit, for a verbal releasing, whether the sun is shining bright with glad rays of hope and faith, or hiding behind projected clouds of doubt or despair, anguish or anger.

Yet if you remain in prayer granting it the time it needs to catch up with the invisible space, prayer alone opens quick as air to fill your soul; that lowly patch of prayer grass, will transition into a vehicle meant for flight.

Better still, prayer will at last be grasped for what it truly is: a magic carpet, designed from above, to take you where it wills, to unmask sights and sounds, tastes and touches not of this place.

Prayer's magic carpet will lift you to sacred space reserved for you alone, as your personal abode of being in relationship with the beyond.

Prayer's comforting carpet will take you where you secretly already are, which upon arriving you will find is your destined space to share with God.

If you pray this meditative prayer, over time—God's time—sooner or later, you will experience holy "liftoff." And inexplicably, you will fly to where you secretly already are, hidden from the world with God.

YOU ALREADY LOVE GOD

YOU ALREADY LOVE GOD. You just may not yet know it. But when you finally encounter God, you will discover love for God already present in you as a gift, which has been waiting to surface and change your life. That will be the time your life with God shall truly begin, for which there will be no ending, both here and in heaven.

In a related context, it is rightly said that you cannot help but love your mother and father, even if they have disappointed and wounded you. Regardless of any anger, distrust, or possibly disgust, beneath all that is an unrequited love. Nor can you finally and forever close your heart to your parents, though you may think you have. That love is still in you, frustrated, tormented, and seemingly lost. Yet forgiveness always remains a possibility, even should you refuse to go there right now. I have seen too many reconciliations between adult children and their parents to doubt this reality.

So it may well be with God, your true and eternal Parent. This is the case no matter what wounds life may have inflicted upon you. There is no wound heaven cannot and will not heal; and if not here, then in heaven.

I discovered this hidden love already living in me when God drew near and embraced me in God's unspeakable yet undeniable way. Here is my prayer describing this blessed event:

I loved you before I knew you. When you dawned upon me, the rays of you reached at first light all that I am, all that I have been, all that I shall be. And I knew then there was never a time I did not love you, nor could there ever be a time I would not love you.

I love you because you loved me first. My love arose in response to yours, arose uncreated, unbidden, unmatched, arose as a flower-strewn path to you fixed before the foundations of the world.

I loved you from the first moment of your glimmering grace. I loved you from the first with a love that lifted me, carried me to you, a love that knew not only you but the way to you, a love that found not only you but me in finding you.

In my love for you, hidden in me, hidden from me from the beginning, was also hidden the stilled shrine of the knowledge of you. When you dawned, you summoned forth my love and knowledge as twin gifts for me and for us, forever.

This love is already in you, waiting to arise like a priceless flower of sheer delight in God, from the soil of your soul. When God draws near to you in prayer, you will undergo a simultaneous event of the utmost importance. The "who" of God, and the "how" of your love for God will meet and merge, so that you will not be able to think of the one without the other.

ON LOVING CHRIST

Do you love Jesus Christ? I mean for who Christ is, rather than for what Christ can do for you? Here is dialogue which occurred unexpectedly between Christ and me about this issue:

The Lord said to me, "Do you love Me for my power or my Person, for what I can do for you, or for who I am to you?"

The tenderest of questions, the opened heart of the One asking, waiting to hear from the heart of the addressed, requiring the most honest of answers—with my future possibly at stake in my reply.

A test I did not seek found me; a question I did not want to be put before me had nevertheless been tossed like a gauntlet at my feet.

So I said to the Lord, "I am in awe of your power, but I am in love with your Person; I dare not fall in love with power, along with its corrupting excesses.

"Show apart from substance does not impress, and your substance is love itself.

"I ask for your power to protect loved ones, to heal and comfort those in need, but I do not love your power, even when it has shown its holy, humble face.

"I love the doer rather than the deed, the worker rather than the work.

"I do not daily meditate on you for your power, but for the nearness of your person.

"I want to remain in a heart union with you without end.

Does this answer your question, beloved?"

And the Lord said to me:

"I hide evidence of my power here; I want those who pursue me to do so with the desire for me rather than my benefits.

Those who search for me with their whole hearts, I let find me.

Have I not let you find me? That is your answer."

249

How we feel toward Christ matters more than what we do for Christ. Remember what the resurrected Jesus asked the apostle Peter three successive times—after Peter had earlier denied knowing him three times—"Do you love me?" And after each time Peter said "yes," the Lord commanded him to "Tend [or feed] my sheep" (John 21:15–17). Love comes before mission, so that mission is always founded and built on love.

God looks to the heart above all. And you can always ask for more love from and for God. All you need is a desire to love God for God. Ask God to increase your love for Jesus Christ as well as your awareness of that love. Breathe in Christ's love for you, and breathe out your love for Christ. Remember that "we love because he first loved us" (1 John 4:19). Seek simply to return God's love made sweeter by your own love in response.

Ask for more love, coming to you, and arising from you. That is the same thing as asking God for more of God.

THE TOUCH OF GOD

THERE IS NO GREATER gift in prayer than the touch of God. It is both indescribable and undeniable; you know at once that it is God, and that it is strangely familiar to you. And when God touches you, it is from the inside. No one but God can do that. It is always the touch of immeasurable love. And as the hymn "He Touched Me" says, God's touch will heal your soul and make you whole. Truly, God loves you in your totality, even if you do not.

The wondrous touch of God will bring forth the fruit of the Spirit, which Paul says includes: "love, joy, peace, patience, kindness, generosity, faithfulness, gentleness, and self-control" (Gal 5:22). These all come at once in varying degrees, depending on your readiness to accept, embrace, and live out of these fruit.

God prefers to touch you softly, tenderly, like a mother her child or a lover their beloved. And God seems to desire that you become sensitive to God's gentle touch, without fear; and that you trust God's touch completely, trust that God will never hurt or reject you. God knows as no one else where and when and how you need to be touched, even if you did not realize it until God's actual touch.

Here is my attempt to describe if not God's touch, at least its effects on me:

You have touched me, more gently than the breeze can caress the tenderest new buds in the forests of the dawning day.

You have touched me, with more love than a mother can feel as she glides her fingers across her newborn's feeling skin.

You have touched me, with more understanding of my frame than lovers can attain in the hungering unions of the night.

When you touched me, you birthed the lover in me, living now for your touch, your nearness, your breath upon me.

When you touched me, you silenced forever the critic, the cynic in me, silenced the little mind building boxcars, instead sitting in them with doors open, beholding the moving scenes of a creation greater than logic can imagine, let alone encompass.

I suggest you begin your meditative prayer with these words: "Lord touch me in whatever way you chose, in whatever way I am ready to receive. Help me to trust your touch completely, and to remain open to your love long enough to be gratefully satisfied with your way with me. Amen." Call it the ultimate "trust fall" into God. You could even imagine such a fall backwards, into the waiting arms of ultimate love.

THE BREATH OF GOD

IN ONE OF THE most dramatic, significant,and yet intimate, tender moments of the Gospels, the resurrected Jesus breathes the Holy Spirit onto His gathered disciples: "Jesus said to them again, 'Peace be with you. As the Father has sent me, so I send you.' When he had said this, he breathed on them and said to them, 'Receive the Holy Spirit. If you forgive the sins of any, they are forgiven them; if you retain the sins of any, they are retained'" (John 20:21–23).

Can you imagine what it must have been like to have Christ's own breath, the very breath of God, the Holy Spirit, gently blown into your face, lungs, and heart? Life-changing for sure. God breathed on me once, and this is how I later depicted this truly indescribable event:

Once you breathed on me; I felt your breath, so softly surrounding me, then slowing, ever so delicately, moving through and filling me with your liberating presence.

Then your breath became you, how I know not, but when your breath morphed into you it ceased to move; everything ceased moving within and around me.

There was simple union, pure you and only you for a space as immeasurable as it was unforgettable.

You are Spirit; you are love; light and airy, yet of greater substance and power than all the mass and energy generated by your big bang.

This is but one of your paradoxes:

Ultimate power one with ultimate tenderness, strength wed inseparably to gentleness.

You are yourself the miracle of all miracles.

Breathe on me, breath of God; transform my weighted being into your weightless wind, blowing wherever it will, in accordance with your will, knowing your freedom of flight.

One of my favorite hymns is "Breathe on Me, Breath of God," written by Edwin Hatch in 1878. Here are its four verses, slightly modernized. As you meditate on these heartfelt words, pray that God will breathe on you, establishing in you the spiritual truths they contain:

1. Breathe on me, Breath of God, fill me with life anew, that I may love the way you love, and do what you would do.

2. Breathe on me, Breath of God, until my heart is pure, until my will is one with yours, to do and to endure.

3. Breathe on me, Breath of God, until I am wholly yours, until this earthly part of me glows with your fire divine.

4. Breathe on me, Breath of God, so shall I never die, but live with You the perfect life of Your eternity.

THE GAZE OF GOD

WHEN GOD GAZES UPON you, God takes in the whole of your past, present, and even future. As the psalmist recognized with a shudder, "For it was you who formed my inward parts; you knit me together in my mother's womb. I praise you, for I am fearfully and wonderfully made. Wonderful are your works; that I know very well. My frame was not hidden from you, when I was being made in secret, intricately woven in the depths of the earth. Your eyes beheld my unformed substance. In your book were written all the days that were formed for me, when none of them as yet existed" (Ps 139:13–16).

Once I sensed the silent gaze of God, penetrating to the hitherto unknown depths of my soul, as if to bring everything I was, am, and shall be to the yielding surface of my consciousness. I wrote:

Once during prayer, God gazed upon me, how I know not, only that God was focusing on my entire being with a totality only God can attain.

Everything slowed down to stoppage, except my breath, as I somehow was granted the sight to follow God's gaze, looking at my past, present, and future.

God saw all I have been and done, the highs and lows, loves and hates, the moments of tenderness and violence.

And as I said, "Please forgive me," I sensed a release only God can grant.

Then God gazed upon my present being, and saw much more to me than I had imagined; I deepened my breath, as if to take in all that God saw in me, as me with God, not as a thing-in-myself.

God affirmed what only God can see.

Finally, God looked to my future, as if it were a single path of God's design and destiny for me.

A light from above suddenly shone on my indeterminate tomorrows, and I heard God's whispered voice calling, summoning me forth with a simple address:

"Hal!" rang the divine imperative, as only God can speak.

Henceforth, the whole of my being, past, present, and future has been gathered up into God, and my journey into tomorrow God called and confirmed, and as only God can, blessed.

Pray that God gaze upon you in a manner that reveals God's utterly true insight to you. Ask that you be permitted to sense what God sees; and trust that in the end, you too will feel forgiven, loved, and blessed.

THE TRUTHS OF GOD

WHATEVER ELSE I AM, I am a seeker after truth. Wherever that leads me, there I will go. Like a loving spouse, I want to be ever faithful to truth. I detest lies and half-truths, and the evil one, whom Jesus calls "a liar and the father of lies" (John 8:44). There are numerous lies and deceptions out there today, many of which serve only to divide and turn us against each other.

We must turn to God for truth and unity. God *is* ultimate truth, and God's truths are imperishable. When God draws near, radiant light shines in the darkness, which can neither comprehend nor overpower it. And we can finally see and feel the truths of God. Jesus Christ not only brought us truth, but *is* God's truth, truth about not only God, but also about us and our destiny in Christ. Jesus said, "You will know the truth, and the truth will make you free" (John 8:32), and "I am the way, and the truth, and the life" (John 14:6). Jesus three times called the Holy Spirit, whom he came to give us, "the Spirit of truth" (John 14:17; 15:26; 16:13). The Spirit offers us calming clarity and affirming assurance in an anxious world.

Today there is far too little faithfulness, loyalty, or the knowledge of God in the land (Hos 4:1). When have we ever had a greater need for the knowledge of God in our land? Not just knowing the biblical truths of how to live and love God and our neighbor, but of persons who have actually experienced God, learned firsthand the who of God?

When God draws near in prayer, God will indeed set you free from falsehood and fear. God will grant you a clarity available only in prayer. Here is the deal: we live in an "as if" world, as if certain things are true which may not be. God brings the "as is" domain of heaven. Among the truths which God will communicate to you in prayer, without needing words, are these:

> *I am real and with you always . . .*
> *I made you and you are mine . . .*
> *I know you as no other . . .*

257

I love you as no other . . .

I am pleased with you . . .

I will never abandon or reject you . . .

I will take you to myself, that we may be together forever . . .

Do not fear, for I am greater than the universe and your future is assured in me.

God can instantly implant these truths into your soul with a mere breath or tender touch of "the Spirit of truth." Once you have encountered God's inviolate truths, your singular task will be to trust in them, as in God.

OPEN THE GIFT YOU ARE

YOU ARE GOD'S GIFT to yourself. That may sound strange, but it is nonetheless the truth. As I wrote to myself back in my twenties, shortly after my first encounter with the Holy Spirit, "God gave me, me, long before I asked." By that I meant there was more to me than I had imagined, that my true self is the one God made me to be from my very beginning, and silently sees me as being. Though I still remain a mystery to myself, I have been assured that whoever I am, I am God's.

Built on that realization, my calling from God, in addition to loving the God who loves me, and my neighbor as myself, is to love myself. And to do so for God's sake even above my own. To love yourself as God's creation includes opening your gifts and talents, and believing in and developing the gift you are to God, to others, and to yourself.

As Rabbi Hillel, an older contemporary of Jesus, famously said, "If I am not for me, who is? And if not now, when? But if I am only for myself, what am I?"

And so I say, "Open the gift you are!" Here is a mediation with that title:

Open the gift you are, to yourself and others, the gift from God, given long before you could ask.

You already are who you long to be, in ways that only you can discern, potential, actual, becoming, being, all of the above, all at once. In the seed is already the tree waiting to unfold and expand its giftedness to itself and the yielding forests of distinguished otherness.

Untie the bow of being, open the box of divine surprises, be fully, joyously the one who pops up and out.

Seek not to repress, suppress, or depress the one you cannot help but be.

Seek not yourself from others; you have already received you from the only one who truly matters.

You are the gift God intended you to be.

You just need to unfurl your inner being with the gentle fingers of faith, hope, and love, for there can be no other you but you, which you must choose to be in the quieting conviction that God has already blessed you with you as a sheer gift of grace, welcoming you to life.

As you meditate on being God's gift to yourself, let self-acceptance arise and strengthen in you. The truth is, if you do not accept yourself, both known and yet unknown, you are in effect saying "no" to God's birthing gift of you. Yet God will patiently await your self-discovery, leading to self-recovering.

THE DARKNESS

WE ARE CALLED BY the light of eternity to be the light of the world. We tend to view darkness as evil, since evil much prefers darkness to light. Yet darkness is as light to God, who sees equally in both temporal domains. As the psalmist said, in utter awe of the omnipresent, all-knowing God: "If I say, 'Surely the darkness shall cover me, and the light around me become night,' even the darkness is not dark to you; the night is as bright as the day, for darkness is as light to you" (Ps 139:11–12). It was God, after all, who formed light and darkness (Isa 45:7).

As a child, I feared the darkness, or at least what might be hidden in the darkness. I comforted myself with Psalm 23:4 "Yea, though I walk through the valley of the shadow of death, I will fear no evil: for thou art with me; thy rod and thy staff they comfort me" (KJV). While in the Marine Corps as a young man, I continued to comfort myself with these assuring words. And in the times I came across and then against evil, I always sought to shine the light of God, of truth and justice, to chase away the evil one, who dwells in darkness.

After a period of nearly five years of spiritual intimacy with God, the door to communion was abruptly closed, without explanation. Just before the door closed, the voiceless echo of God said: "It will not always be like this." Then I entered what St. John of the Cross, a sixteenth-century Christian mystic, called "the dark night of the soul." It happened right at the time I entered seminary and the ministry. I felt rejected and constantly prayed for a return to the "salad days" of romantic love with the beloved. I felt like a rejected lover. I had—and have—no power over God; God is ever in charge, and sets the agenda. I begged God to be permitted to come in from the cold, to reengage in our intimacy. I feared that I may have done something wrong, or gotten too used to our mutuality. I asked for forgiveness constantly. But nothing availed me.

Thirty-one years later, during a ten-day intensive centering prayer retreat, the dark night broke with the dawning of a heart-to-heart union with

Jesus Christ. A few years later, during my morning prayer, Christ said something to me that changed my understanding of what I had lived through. The words came without preparation or fanfare: "I was closer to you in the darkness than you thought I was in the light." I sensed the truth of these words immediately. Responding to Christ's words, I wrote:

In the darkness, I have no other sense than you; you bring your sense, like a scent, with you, as calling card and gift.

In the darkness, no sights or sounds to distract my heart's desire for you ascending like an arrow knowing the whereabouts of its intended target;

Being pierced, my heart seeks to pierce your heart, building then a line of love between this and the other side, never to be severed, but ever to serve us as ours alone.

Forgive me, beloved, if I long to wound you with the love by which you have wounded me, as if our commonality might guarantee a common future.

Do not fear the darkness. God may be or abide in absolute light; yet the darkness and whatever dwells in the darkness are not hidden from God. When you pray, take with you the faith that God will be closer to you in the darkness than in the light. Trust and live the words of the psalmist, "The LORD is my light and my salvation; whom shall I fear? The LORD is the stronghold of my life; of whom shall I be afraid?" (Ps 27:1).

AWAKENING

I PLACE THIS MEDITATION prayer here because it transitions from meditating to contemplating, from praying to sense God to actually encountering the Spirit of God. Titled "Awakening," it is as close as I have come to describing the ineffable event of union with God, albeit temporary in time, though not in effect. It is an allegory, but a somewhat accurate one.

I invite you to come along with me and meditate on an inland sea. Find an imaginative place from which to visualize stilled water, whether from the shore or from a boat, drifting atop its inviting and silent surface. When the unseen God draws near, both your heart and the water will stir to announce the holy. If and when that happens, do not fear, but open freely, fully, and fondly to the beloved one whom you already know, yet forgot until such an awakening moment:

Meditating on a calmed inland sea, letting go and letting be before its beckoning presence, my heart stirs at an approaching other.

I can but wait in hushed stillness, breathing in the salted air of promise, sensing that something is about to be.

From the edges of my awareness arises a summoned wave of focused water washing me overboard into itself.

Pulled deeper and deeper by a power unseen, into a strangely breathable darkening water, encircled and caressed by ineffable bubbles of life and love, I leave language behind on the fading surface.

All motion ceases:

Floating now in the depths of peace, engulfed completely by the knowing water, I yield myself to its naked now, an unexpected home in the first place.

Losing myself in what has found me, with no lingering self-concern, I simply am, in what I am, with whom I am.

After a time between the seconds, I find myself on a humbled shore, dry but awakened, walking along the lonely sands of driftwood memories.

You may seek but cannot enter the waters of the Spirit of God without God parting those waters and guiding you in. God will do so when you are ready. Let your desire for God and the wondrous waters of the Spirit increase. Loose your hungering heart to fly arrow-like toward God, for it is born knowing the way. If such a desire bursts forth in you, do not tarry, do not let shyness, doubt, or uncertainty delay you. Show God by your persistence that it is "God or bust."

CONTEMPLATIVE PRAYER

"Contemplative prayer is natural, unprogrammed; it is perpetual openness to God, so that in the openness his concerns can flow in and out of our minds as he wills."

—RAY SIMPSON

"Contemplative prayer removes us from the driver's seat."

—ED CYZEWSKI

"Prayer does not change God; prayer changes us. God is perfect and constant—absolute. We pray to experience God."

—ELIZABETH C. DIXON

ABOUT CONTEMPLATIVE PRAYER

WE COME TO THE final and ultimate stage of prayer in this life: contemplation. You are ready for contemplative prayer when your heart seeks to commune with God directly, when nothing and no one but God will satisfy you. Psalm 73:24–26 well expresses this life-changing realization: "Whom have I in heaven but you? And there is nothing on earth that I desire other than you. My flesh and my heart may fail, but God is the strength of my heart and my portion forever."

Contemplative prayer is a heart-to-heart communion, which begins when you seek God for God. You will likely not be aware of the depth of your desire for God at first. It's like drinking water when you do not know how thirsty you are until you swallow that first drink. Then you discover the extent of your deeper thirst, right along with the joy of the water. The psalmist poignantly realizes this in Psalm 63:1: "O God . . . I seek you, my soul thirsts for you; my flesh faints for you, as in a dry and weary land where there is no water."

The singular aim of contemplative prayer is direct connection with God, with the mysterious "who" of God. It is built on desire and is always heart-led, since only the heart knows the way. Prayer becomes mystical when God enters into your private prayer-space. God then turns your thirsting aloneness into overflowing mutuality. God does so in a wordless embrace of being by being, like a transforming hug beyond language.

Contemplation is a sheer gift of God. It is God's work in and with you, which can be taught only by God. God will do so in God's timing and way, when God determines you are ready to enter into God. As the medieval Christian mystic Meister Eckhart said, "You can only experience God in God's own space."

Contemplation is the lovemaking that occurs in the marital union between God and humanity. St. Theresa of Avila called such intimate prayer "spiritual sex." It is spiritual, not physical—though the *unio mystica*, or mystical union of your soul to God, will generate profound effects upon your body. Here is an attempt to describe the indescribable, the mystical union with God, the Supreme "Thou" of all life:

You and I have been one, Beloved. We have met and merged, where and how I know not, for in the realm between us, there are no fixed markers or buoys, no stable stars or shores by which to determine our whereabouts.

We met in heaven, we met on earth, we met in me, we met in you, all of these all at once. More than that I cannot say. Our where is as great a mystery as your who.

I cannot say how long we were one, for though there was a filled duration, the time of our meeting was as indeterminable as its space. It does not matter how long you and I were one, but that we were one. What matters is that you happened to me, that the shutter snapped, the imprint took, my soul expanded to receive you.

I cannot say by what means I knew you, but it was you, only you, ever you that I knew. You alone were the content; nothing could be taken from the wholeness of your holiness.

I did not know myself, I knew only you, as if your consciousness absorbed mine, as if my consciousness had become a fiery fragment of yours, as if I were no longer a separate soul, but a common cup for sharing you, the one God.

The miracle of knowing you, of merging with you, was succeeded by the miracle of coming back to myself, of becoming again a singular dwelling, once the flood of you receded.

Instead of becoming you, which will never happen, I shared you, which will ever be my fondest joy and greatest hope.

Words cannot describe the event of the *unio mystica*. The anonymous medieval writer of one of the most important works on mystical union said that meeting and merging with God could only happen in the "Cloud of Unknowing," which is also the title of the book. In that indescribable cloud, you both know and yet do not and cannot know in the sense of gaining a describable knowledge of an object or event in the world. It is rather like trying to describe light to someone born totally blind. Nevertheless, I offer this attempt to put into words something of my contemplative prayer life with God.

In this final division of this prayer book, I will attempt the impossible. I will seek to put words to what my life with God as a contemplative has been and remains. Every section originates from my own relationship with God. But be assured that once you have encountered the beloved, the truth of these sections will come alive. It will be like finally hearing the music, after merely reading the score. It will be the relational moment when a monologue becomes a dialogue, when your attention shifts from you and what you want to say to God, on to God and what God may be saying to you, with a message felt more than heard, deeper than words can articulate. It will change your life forever. Once you become a contemplative, you will always be a contemplative.

THE GOD HUG

HAVE YOU EVER WANTED to be hugged by someone who truly loves you, whom you genuinely trust? Imagine being hugged by love itself, hugged in your completeness, soul as well as body. Mystical union begins as a desire for that hug, that holy embrace. It is as simple as it is profound. It includes a vivid sense of the "who" of God loving the who of you.

Words cannot adequately describe how it feels to be hugged by a loved one. Imagine the hug of God, hugging your inner being, your true self in its totality. That may be the closest analogy to the mystical union with God. Contemplative prayer seeks the touch, if not the hug of God. Once God hugs you in your completeness, you will never forget it; it will change your life forever. And when you long for God, you secretly long to be held by God, "like a weaned child with its mother" (Ps 131:2), in the calming trust and assurance that all will be well, eternally.

I remember a young man I counseled. In our first session, he silently leaned forward, hid his face behind his hands, and began weeping. He cried out: "No one has touched me in years."

I understood his pain. Yet most fortunately, I have been blessed by the touch, the silent hug of God. It was God pure and simple, loving me in a way and to an extent I will never deserve nor understand. It was as if God gave God's Self to me, for an indeterminable time. The God who is love was just there, cleaving to me, as I sought to cleave to God. God's self-giving humbled me to my depths, becoming the foundational pylons of my life.

I attempted to thank God with these meager words:

What you gave me was yourself, not truths, rites, or rituals. No laws, rules, or regulations came along with your coming. You presented only yourself to me, as if to say, "Here I am; I am who I am; I will be to you what I will be."

You are quite the greatest gift of all, the gift which cannot be anticipated, prepared for, deserved. Your nearness alone set me free; your nearness alone imparted the truth that satisfies.

What you gave me was yourself, the best came first, setting in motion the rest of my life. You are the measure of my days, the grounding of my desires, the horizon of my tomorrows.

In giving yourself to me, you gave me heaven right away, from the beginning; with you, I am already where I am going.

The gentle hug of God will strengthen that which is the most tender, the most vulnerable, and the neediest dimension of your soul. Though it is beyond words, when you pray, ask and wait for the touch, the hug of God. No matter how long it takes to receive God's embrace, it will be well worth the wait.

ABIDING PRAYER

GOD HAS TAUGHT ME a contemplative form of prayer which I practice every morning, and during brief periods throughout the day. I call it abiding prayer, and it is based on Jesus' directing us to: "Abide in me as I abide in you . . . Abide in my love" (John 15:4, 9). Abiding prayer is less something you do, and more something you permit to happen. That means abiding prayer is God's prayer in and with you, built on Christ's own insistent directive.

The focus of abiding prayer is on Christ and entering into a heart-to-heart mutual life with Christ *during the prayer itself*. Abiding prayer offers a pathway toward attaining what Christ fervently prays for all disciples: "that they may be one, as we are one, I in them and you in me, that they may become completely one" (John 17:22–23).

Abiding prayer seeks to act on Jesus Christ's direct invitation to abide in him through the Holy Spirit. The center around which abiding prayer revolves is Christ: his person, presence, power, and love. It is Christ who says: "Abide in me as I abide in you . . . Abide in my love." To abide in Christ and his love includes abiding in the Holy Spirit, and in the Trinity as such.

To use an analogy: two magnets and a magnetic field. When a positive and negative magnet become proximate to each other, a magnetic field is generated between them. The two poles seek to unify as one. Just so, your heart will become as a magnet when God draws near; it will stir as a spiritual field is generated between you and God. To abide means to remain in that field between your heart and Christ's heart. That field *is* the Holy Spirit of God's love.

What is sought in abiding prayer is beyond words or images: it is pure presence and togetherness with and in God. You may begin with words and images, but during the silent time of mutual life, when the field has come to exist between you and God, you will sense God with you. You will not likely sense God's approach, but when your heart begins to stir, God is there.

Here is the process of abiding prayer:

1. Begin by granting permission for God's presence and action within you.

2. Sit comfortably in a straight-back chair, with both feet on the ground, hands on thighs and your eyes closed (although if you prefer, you may keep your eyes open).

3. Imagine Jesus being with you, perhaps sitting right across from you. Hear him calmly address you, repeatedly: "Abide in me as I abide in you. Abide in my love." Rather than you initiating the prayer, imagine that you are instead hearing and responding to Christ's words of invitation to intimacy and love. Give Jesus time to make this real and sensed for you. You may in time come to reduce Christ's address to a single word, which will convey the substance of Christ's invitation and your heartfelt acceptance: "abide."

4. Hold on to the word "abide" as if it is issuing between you and Christ. Let your heart's raw desire for God and union with Christ propel you toward and keep you invested in, attaining, and remaining with and in Christ. You can let this become a breath prayer around the word "abide." If so, simply breathe in "Abide in me," and breathe out "As I abide in you."

5. When thoughts, feelings, images, or desires distract you, ever so gently return your attention to Jesus and his inviting words: "Abide in me as I abide in you . . . Abide in my love." Do not get upset with yourself about these distractions, as they come to us all. Learn to let them pass without resisting them, and then return to abiding.

6. After about twenty minutes of prayer, ask Christ to continue abiding with and in you and you with Christ. Following a time of calm reflection, open your eyes.

TEN FOUNDATIONAL BELIEFS ABIDING PRAYER CONFIRMS

THERE IS MORE TO abiding prayer than merely a way of praying. There are foundational beliefs that this prayer confirms. They are fixed, like the stars in the heavens. They shine brightly every time you enter into the comforting vastness of abiding prayer. The ten beliefs are:

1. Christ exists.

"Jesus said to them, 'Very truly, I tell you, before Abraham was, I am'" (John 8:58).

2. Christ is both human and divine.

"The Father and I are one. . . . Whoever has seen me has seen the Father. . . . Believe me that I am in the Father and the Father is in me" (John 10:30; 14:9, 11).

3. Christ has God's power and authority.

"All authority in heaven and on earth has been given to me" (Matt 28:18).

Christ is called "the power of God and the wisdom of God" (1 Cor 1:24).

4. Christ can be known.

"In a little while the world will no longer see me, but you will see me; because I live, you also will live. On that day you will know that I am in my Father, and you in me, and I in you" (John 14:19–20).

5. Christ is with you and in you.

"And remember, I am with you always, to the end of the age" (Matt 28:20).

"To them God chose to make known how great among the Gentiles are the riches of the glory of this mystery, which is Christ in you, the hope of glory" (Col 1:27).

6. Christ knows and loves you.

"I am the good shepherd. I know my own and my own know me" (John 10:14).

"You did not choose me but I chose you. And I appointed you to go and bear fruit, fruit that will last, so that the Father will give you whatever you ask him in my name" (John 15:16).

7. Christ wants you to know and love him.

"They who have my commandments and keep them are those who love me; and those who love me will be loved by my Father, and I will love them and reveal myself to them (John 14:21).

8. Christ seeks to make a home in your heart.

"Those who love me will keep my word, and my Father will love them, and we will come to them and make our home with them" (John 14:23).

"Listen! I am standing at the door, knocking; if you hear my voice and open the door, I will come in to you and eat with you, and you with me" (Rev 3:20).

9. Christ wants to abide in you and have you abide in Christ forever.

"Abide in me as I abide in you. Just as the branch cannot bear fruit by itself unless it abides in the vine, neither can you unless you abide in me. I am the vine, you are the branches. Those who abide in me and I in them bear much fruit, because apart from me you can do nothing . . . As the Father has loved me, so I have loved you; abide in my love" (John 15:4–5, 9).

10. The real presence of Christ shall be known in the heart, as in the Holy Eucharist. Abiding prayer is an essential aid to discerning—and loving—the real presence of Jesus Christ.

CENTERING PRAYER

BEFORE BEING LED INTO abiding prayer, my daily practice was centering prayer. I am certified to teach it, and have led the one-day training course on multiple occasions. Centering prayer is based on an anonymous book written by a masterful spiritual director in England in the fourteenth century. Titled *The Cloud of Unknowing*, it offers succinct direction for those seeking direct, mystical encounters with God. The singular content of such prayer is the person of God.

I am most grateful for centering prayer, and for having encountered God in this "Cloud of Unknowing." In praise of the One who may be experienced but not described, I wrote:

Apart from your Spirit I do not have the words, I cannot find the way to express what I feel, what I sense in me and between us.

When you come you bring the equipment that makes not only communion in Spirit possible, but also communion in word.

How wondrous, O God, that in your grace you not only draw near, not only awaken us to your presence, but also give us the words to address you.

I discern the supportive currents of your Spirit breathing through my breath, returning to you through my prayer.

How great an honor, how great a deed, to yield back to you what belongs to you, coming through, and I hope enriched by, the grateful vessel of my soul breathing love for you.

There are three basic steps to centering prayer:

1. Sit comfortably in a straight-back chair, with both feet on the ground and your hand on your thighs. Settling down, turn your attention to God as you understand God. Consent to God's presence and action within you. Trust that "it is God who is at work in you, enabling you both to will and to work for his good pleasure" (Phil 2:13). Close your eyes if you wish.

2. Choose a single word signifying your heart's desire to encounter God. Cling to that word, as if it were an arrow shot Godward. Silently continue repeating that word at a calm rate.

3. Whenever your mind wanders and you get distracted, simply repeat your sacred word, to ever so gently bring your attention back to God.

Seek to engage in this prayer for twenty minutes at a time, minimally once but optimally twice a day. It may not seem to have much content; but then, your sole objective is to sense the presence of God. And I assure you, that eventually happens to most all of those who persevere in this anointed form of prayer. And the positive changes that can occur may be noticed more by others than by yourself.

THE ROMANCE OF GOD

AT SOME POINT IN your prayer life with God, you will realize that your desire has become romantic. You find yourself seeking "the One" designed for your heart. Bernard of Clairvaux (1090–1153) recognized this long ago. Based on the *Song of Songs* (1:2)—"Let him kiss me with the kisses of his mouth!"—he described the spiritual progression to God in terms of "three kisses."

The first kiss is of God's feet. You begin by recognizing your sinfulness. To prostrate yourself before God is to humble yourself by the realization of your need for God's forgiveness. And you must kiss both of God's feet. One foot represents God's judgment, and the other God's mercy. Here God is your Sovereign, who will determine your destiny. You beg God for mercy and wait in hope for God to say, "You are forgiven." Christ's sacrifice has made that available.

When the Sovereign God announces, "You are forgiven," it generates a desire to become a better person. That desire is one of God's gifts, enabling you to slowly rise toward resting on your knees. Once on your knees, you next kiss God's gracious hands in humble gratitude. Now God is your Father, your Mother. One hand represents God's ever-giving grace, the other God's ever-supporting goodness, strengthening you in your progression upward.

After the second kiss, what prompts the final stage is the desire for God. Now you find yourself longing for the third kiss, the kiss of God's mouth. *The romance of God has begun*; now God is your beloved; now you are as a bride seeking the kiss of the bridegroom. Yet you cannot receive the kiss of God's mouth on your lips and live. You have to wait until you pass over into the "bridal chambers" of heaven for the consummation of your romantic love for God.

Once you are standing, St. Bernard says it is God the beloved who kisses; it is Christ the lover who receives the kiss; and it is the Holy Spirit who *is* the love which kisses. What you may receive in this life is the kiss of the Spirit and the word of God on your cheeks. This is a satisfying down payment on what is to come. Bernard also says that Christ kisses back, returns the love of the beloved, and that this circle is eternal: God the Father eternally kisses God the Son, with the kiss of the Holy Spirit; and Christ returns the kiss, which thus is shared forever between them.

And in and with Christ, you will share in that eternal romance.

Trust that when God draws near, it will be "love at first sight." And at the same time, you will also discover who you are when you are with God. That was my experience, never to be forgotten or transcended. I prayed to God, as a lover to the beloved:

I am only truly alive when you are with me. I am only fully myself in the anointed freedom of your presence.

When we are apart, I so easily forget who I am with you. When you come, you bring me with you. My memory returns as you restore me to myself.

I long to remember and remain who I am with you.

WORDLESS PRAYER

NOT ALL PRAYER REQUIRES words. Indeed, some prayers or portions of prayer require silence to unfold satisfactorily. Such is contemplative prayer. It is a bit like hugging a loved one. There comes a time when words alone will not satisfy the urge of the heart for direct contact and expression of love. Love can be communicated in a wordless hug with a depth and immediacy words alone simply cannot express. And any words spoken while hugging a loved one matter more and hit the heart more directly and deeply than words without a hug, or without a touch.

While in prayer, to hear anything the Spirit might say to you, it is essential that you enter into openhearted, wordless listening, with stilled expectations. This has also been termed "listening with the ear of your heart." The heart may sense or "hear" what the mind cannot receive. Attempting to speak to and listen for God at the same time is a fretful example of "multitasking," something we cannot successfully do with God any more than with another person.

So what does the heart listen for, in its wordless openness to God? It listens for God's subtle, silent, and surprisingly savoring touch. Yes, God does savor; that is, God cherishes your soul-life. If not, you would not be at all. Yet if you are too busy with your own thoughts and wishes and agenda, you will miss God's desire of and agenda for you.

I have been blessed by God's wordless prayer touch. And I have written:

Tenderly, how tenderly have you come upon me in our brief seasons of silent communion, You in me, and I in you. You have touched my soul more surely, more serenely than fingers can caress flesh.

I have experienced you experiencing me as none other, knowing just where and when and how I needed to be touched, wanted to be touched, even if I did not know it until You touched me.

The way you seemed to succor and savor me—what can I say to you, do for you in response, other than say how I love you, how I praise you for your way with me?

Would that I could touch you as you have touched me. Would that I could caress your Spirit as you have caressed my soul.

Let your desire for God expand your heart. God will do so, when you are both awake and asleep. Listen for God in the way your flesh awaits a gentle breeze on a bright summer's day.

THE TWO WAYS

THERE ARE TWO BASIC ways to encounter God. They are mediated and unmediated. The former may be understood as "light" and the latter as "darkness." This is akin to the "yin and yang" vision of Daoism, signifying "darkness and light," respectively. Mediated encounters with God are through some medium, such as nature, art, music, words, and other persons. For a biblical example, the psalmist says, "The heavens are telling the glory of God; and the firmament proclaims his handiwork" (Ps 19:1). Icons can also grant us a sense of the "who" of God and "what" of heaven. These are all manifestations of the unseen God, through which we may experience something of God, like Moses encountering God through the medium of a burning bush. God was neither *in* the burning bush, nor synonymous *with* it. Rather, God used the bush as a medium of revelation. God spoke *through* it.

It is however, through the unmediated way that we may encounter God more directly, without the aid of some means through which to describe something about God. Here stillness and silence reign, as in: "Be still, and know that I am God" (Ps 46:10). The unmediated way occurs only in the darkness, where words fail to adequately express the absolute uniqueness of God. Though we may use analogies and parables in an effort to delineate the "who" of God, God remains beyond them, and may only be encountered directly whether in the light or in the darkness of prayer.

A similar either/or for how we may encounter God is the "way of affirmation" (called "kataphatic") over against the "way of negation" (called "apophatic"). The former states that God can be portrayed by positive terms like "Father," "Light," "Water," and "Wind." The latter asserts that God cannot be described, that we cannot say what God is, but only what God is not.

I am comfortable with both ways of prayer, and have encountered God in the darkness as well as in the light. Whether through the light of a medium or through the directness only darkness affords, you will know, and know that you know God in an immediacy beyond words. You will know the who of God through God's wondrous gift of *intuition*. As I have written:

I sense you not through myself but only through you. You bring with you the intuition of yourself; and alas, you take it with you when you leave.

Intuition then is a momentary gift belonging only to you, given only while you give yourself to me as I give myself to you, in our fleeting moments of mutual life.

Intuition is not something I do but you do in me, something done for me that I cannot do. It is as if you part the curtains of your hiddenness close by, that through you I may, to an extent beyond measurement, know you as you are knowing me.

Learn to trust the intuition of God, when and as God draws near to you, regardless of whether it is in the light or in the darkness. They are the same to God (Ps 139:12). Pray for greater intuition, so you may sense God all the better.

The truth is, you need both the light and the darkness for a satisfying, fulfilling prayer life with God. You need signs of God's presence, person, and love. Yet it is in the darkness where God may draw nearer to you than your own I.

PURE MUTUALITY

A MUTUAL LOVE RELATIONSHIP with another person offers us life-affirming meaning, purpose, and motivation. And the word "mutual" is as significant as the word "love." It is one thing to love a person and another to be loved as fully as you love. Love seeks a love relationship; it longs for the generation of a shared magnetic-like field, where the hearts of both persons act as the two magnets. Call this invisible reality the "love field." Nobody can see it, not even the loving partners. But it is as real as the love itself. And it is just what our restless hearts relentlessly seek: great love, shared and celebrated.

Amazingly, we are actually invited into a shared love relationship with God, one of pure mutuality. In the "we" with God, both partners contribute, with God's love for us adding to, intensifying our love for God. Through our mutuality with God, we become greater than ourselves, beyond what we could be or offer on our own. *God wills pure mutuality.*

Here is one of my prayer poems expressing my desire for and vision of pure mutuality with God. Pray this, giving God time to gently, silently generate an uplifting sense of an impending mutual life together, which is your final, finest destiny:

Cleave to me, Lord, in my cleaving to you.

Rest upon my soul, as I rest upon your Spirit.

Though you are infinitely greater than I, make a home in my heart, a little oasis of love for you.

I can offer you nothing other than myself, and seek nothing from you other than yourself.

Let there be pure mutuality between us, simply being to Being.

If that is not heaven, nothing else could be.

Finally, here are two Scripture passages to pray along with the above prayer poem:

Because you cleave* to me in love, I will deliver you.

I will protect you, because you know my name.

When you call to me, I will answer you;

I will be with you in trouble,

I will rescue you and honor you.

With long life I will satisfy you,

and show you my salvation. (Ps 91:14–16 RSV paraphrase)

Listen! I am standing at the door, knocking; if you hear my voice and open the door, I will come in to you and eat with you, and you with me. (Rev 3:20)

---

* "Cleave" in the original Hebrew is *devekut*, which means "devotion," signifying cleaving to, as lovers cleave to each other, or as parents and children cleave to one another. Such an intense mutual union is the most profound reason for our existence, as well as our ultimate destiny.

THE DOOR

"Listen! I am standing at the door, knocking; if you hear my voice and open the door, I will come in to you and eat with you, and you with me." (Rev 3:20)

THERE IS A DOOR hidden within your heart which will open only to love, and by love. Twice, one week apart, that door of my heart opened, back in November 1967. The first time the door opened was when the Holy Spirit, the love of God embraced me. The second time, one week to the day later, was when the human love of my life walked through a just-opened physical door. Though both encounters happened suddenly, I must have been ready to receive God as well as my beloved partner. I had been eagerly searching for both God and great love.

Perhaps the readiness really is all. But you will not open that door until the fragrant sense of love invites you to do so. And though you may err about human love, the love of God is for real and forever.

If you are ready, now could be your grand opening. See where this prayer leads you:

You have opened a door in me to another realm, one of utter mystery and beauty.

It is the personal realm of your being, which roused me with a burst of heaven, bringing into my unseen being fresh light and life and love, your light, your life, and your love.

Once you opened that door, with my full, even pleading consent, having waited until my whole heart sought you, I will not, I want not, nor can I close it; it is permanently fixed by your Spirit to remain an open, narrow passageway between you and me, heaven and earth.

How can I describe to others this invisible door within them that opens you to us and us to you?

Call it the "God door," which once opened shall remain open unto infinity.

That door is in all hearts, awaiting our desire and discovery, our appeal to you in response to your secret summons to us, to "Open, please open" the door to the boundless oasis, which is your home, destined to be our home.

Others may deny your existence, and the presence of that door in the human heart between this and the other side, but they are worse than wrong; they are in hidden fact dammed up, closed off in their hardened hearts, out of touch with God and the things of God, above all, the heart's single passageway to union with God and God with us.

THE TEMPLE INVISIBLE

THE UNDERGROUND RIVER OF prayer, arising spontaneously as a spring from the unreachable depths of your heart, flows inevitably into the "temple invisible." It is in this mystical and unsearchable realm where prayer becomes a dialogue rather than monologue, something not just from you, but also from God. Your prayer may begin as you seeking God, but once you enter the temple, you will discover that it is in startling fact God who is seeking you. And God will always find you, when you are ready and desirous of being found by God.

Yet you must be invited to enter the temple invisible. Once there—wherever "there" is—you will not want to leave, period. The temple is the sacred meeting space of God. The air is strangely heightened; the atmosphere is more real then what seems real in this ever enlarging cosmos of time and space. The temple is at once within you, around you, and inexplicably between you and the unseen God. It will feel as if you are somehow sharing in God's own breath.

The immovable temple stands hidden between God and us, between the universe of matter and the universe of Persons, both human and divine. It is the singular meeting place between heaven and earth, this world and the world after, if not also before, this life.

It is in this invisible domain of God where ineffable moments of union with God may occur, as reported by mystics throughout the ages. I, too, have been blessed by such ecstatic events. I have attempted to put words to this glorious yet invisible temple:

I want to build a temple for you in words, a place for you to dwell in listening silence, a place for your Spirit to breathe upon and fill.

Yet all I have to build with are human words, and how inadequate they are to the task: you cannot be put into words or housed in language any more than in stone.

And where temples of whatever sort have been built, idols and image-worship seek to move in like noxious weeds into a garden.

I want to build a tabernacle of language that will last, and not deteriorate or crumble claylike with age.

And I want to plant it in the midst of humanity, as if to point and attend to you.

Yet you have no body, and there is no place you are not.

No matter what words I could use to carve out my gratitude, Beloved, they would fail to lift off the dusty ground of my being as if to hover about you like your adoring cherubim.

Yet all language begins in your word of address, and shall return to you in your timing and way.

I do not want to be silenced by your ineffable presence; I want to say something positive about you besides the stammering utterance: "I love you," which expresses feeling without form.

Perhaps the only temple my words can construct would rest unseen between you and me, built like the covered bridges of old, shadowy yet strangely heightening; a place where mystery could discreetly meet Mystery, and where any words would be for our ears only.

If these words intensify your desire for God, then let the prayer arising spontaneously from your heart, guide you to this secret temple between God and you. God will not refuse your heart's desire. Once in the temple, you will finally find the God who has long sought you.

THE NAMELESS PLACE

I CANNOT ADEQUATELY PUT into words a mystical moment of union with God. Yet I keep attempting to do the impossible. Here is yet another attempt. If you have had such a moment beyond speech with God, you will hopefully get what I am saying. If not, you have that to look forward to, since God's desire for you is far greater than your desire for God, and will continue until it is fulfilled with you.

I enter what enters me, reaching a place in me, yet not in me, releasing me to extend beyond the sensed boundaries of my being alone in the world.

I rest there in your resting in me, my breath taking in and yielding back your breath, rarefying my consciousness by your Spirit-oxygen.

The unspoken in me meets your silent presence, the one not confounding but comforting the other; your vastness expands exponentially the nameless expanse between us.

Nothing is lost but everything is gained.

I have no name for our unseen realm of meeting; to attempt to circumscribe it with a name could seem to reduce you and me and us to graspable conceptual constructs.

Naming inevitably births images, and images risk possible idolatry:
Worshiping the image rather than the one it depicts.

Images remain vulnerable to becoming surrogates for true meeting and mutual abiding.

Naming God does not mean knowing God; naming our hidden place of meeting does not mean entering it.

When I do enter the nameless place, my mouth will shut as my soul opens, to receive and share directly what cannot be put into words.

More than a mere space, which could be empty as well as filled by quantities seeking named recognition, what God opens between us is never empty, nor nameable.

Imagine the freedom of not having to name or explain your meeting place with God to anyone else. If what the poet suggests is true, that a rose by any other name is still a rose, surely that would also apply to God, who refused to give a real name to Moses. Rather, when Moses asked God who he should say sent him to bring back the Israelites, God's answer from the burning bush, silenced him. In Hebrew, God literally said, "I will be to you as I will yet be" (Exod 3:14). This is not really a name, coming from the God who refuses to be bound by anything other than love itself.

God's answer to Moses, however, seems to anticipate a mysterious future relationship not yet ready to be revealed. And Jesus only intensified the mystery of our coming relationship with God with these cryptic words: "I still have many things to say to you, but you cannot bear them now. When the Spirit of truth comes, he will guide you into all the truth; for he will not speak on his own, but will speak whatever he hears, and he will declare to you the things that are to come" (John 16:12–13).

When you seek God in prayer, be open to going where God wants you to go. At some point, your relationship will become romantic, through and through. Maybe even eternally.

THE KISS OF GOD

YOU CAN TELL A lot by a kiss. Certainly whether there is a romantic interest, either on your part or the other. Or more significantly, whether it is on both your parts, opening up a mutual world to explore together. Granted, feelings change; romantic love comes and goes, whether it dissipates and disappears, or morphs into the long-term "real thing." Only time will tell.

God is the hidden matchmaker of romantic love, which is secretly a rehearsal for the eternal romance to come. God is destined to become your eternal beloved (see Hos 2:19–20 and Rev 21:1–2). And talk about love at first sight! This is what the Song of Songs is really about: romantic love between humanity and God, and the discovery of your true and ultimate "other." It begins: "O that you would kiss me with the kisses of your mouth" (1:2).

Saint Bernard of Clairvaux (1090–1153), as we saw earlier, was fascinated with the kiss of God. So much so that he wrote eighty-six sermons on the Song of Songs, but never got past the third chapter. In his grand vision of the romantic love between God and the soul, at the end of our life journey, God will finally kiss us on our lips, something too wonderful for us to withstand while embodied here.

Visualize receiving God's kiss. Pray for it; trust that it is on the way. Here is my desire:

I want to know who you are by a kiss, how you feel toward me, whether what you feel is akin to what I feel, in a kiss.

I seek lips touching, breath ceasing, when I may sense what is between us.

Will I discern love's dance of destined union, stirring my heart and hopes, or will I be met by a holy sovereign, who loves, but not as a lover, not as my heart's beloved?

I cannot do other than seek that kiss, Your mouth meeting mine, experiencing you in your experiencing me, connected at last, being to being, doorway to opened doorway, the sweet draft of desire meeting desire fanning between us.

From where does this desire arise to know you, mouth to mouth, lips to lips, breath to breath?

Does this longing spring from me alone, or from your yearning arousing mine?

Is it your desire that I sense, or only my desire I am projecting onto your blessed countenance?

Only a kiss will tell.

PRAYER FOR JESUS' HEART

IMAGINE HOW IT WOULD feel if, while you were praying, Jesus softly invited you to share his heart. This would inevitably lead to Christ saying: "Your heart and my heart are one." In amazing fact, Christ essentially said that to some medieval Christian mystics. What it means is your heart and the Sacred Heart of Jesus Christ have somehow become connected, intertwined, united. Does that sound strange, maybe even alien to your faith? It should not be; rather, it might be an indication of your distance from the "heart" of the gospel. The epicenter of the gospel, especially the writing of the apostles John and Paul, is our living union with Jesus Christ. And how that union is to come about is as profound as it is simple: heart to heart. And is this not the center and substance of a love relationship like that of marriage? Two hearts conjoined so closely that they nearly beat as one?

At least that is the image, and it is an accurate one. It certainly has been for me. A few years ago, Christ said these words to me, addressing my soul rather than body: "Thy heart is my heart; my heart is thy heart." What that means to me is that I am in an inexplicable but absolutely real and unending union with Christ's heart. I explain this in my 2018 book, *The Heart of Jesus and the Coming Relationship*.

As I have indicated, there were medieval saints who had much the same experience. In fact, Christ apparently said the very same words to Mechthild of Hackeborn (1240–1298). And that may be the real and ultimate mission of Jesus Christ: to wed our hearts with his heart for all eternity. I am convinced that that is our furthest destiny.

Do you know how that is going to happen? On the basis of what God has done in me, Christ's heart will unite with our hearts, healing, renewing, strengthening, and wordlessly assuring us that absolutely nothing "will be able to separate us from the love of God in Christ Jesus our Lord" (Rom 8:39). Heaven includes a heart-to-heart union with Christ.

Treat this as a breath prayer: simply breathe in Christ's loving heart and breathe out your needy heart, almost like the exchange of rings during a wedding ceremony. You are, so to say, giving your hearts to each other. So sitting comfortably in a straight-back chair, feet on the ground, eyes closed, hands on your thighs, breathe in "Your heart" and breathe out, "My heart." Do "belly breathing," and let the relaxed rhythm of your lungs continue, as you address Christ, breathing in, "Your heart" and offering in exchange as you breathe out, "My heart."

Pray this for ten minutes. Hopefully your heart will begin stir as you will slowly sense a magnetic-like connection growing between your heart and the heart of Jesus Christ.

UNION WITH GOD

THE ULTIMATE GOAL OF prayer is union with God. Your understanding of God and what kind of union you seek will evolve as you mature. Yet you can and even must pray honestly from where you are with God now, without concern about the rightness or wrongness of what you seek. God would prefer you to taste a variety of foods before you discover the soul-satisfying food of the feast of divine love.

Ultimately, if you persevere in prayer, you will learn that only God can satisfy your heart's desire for that which is beyond naming. As the psalmist realized: "Whom have I in heaven but you? And there is nothing on earth that I desire other than you. My flesh and my heart may fail, but God is the strength of my heart and my portion forever" (Ps 73:25–26).

Those words mean a lot to me. One of my prayer poems says to be careful for what you ask:

Ask for your blessing, and that is what you may give, but only your blessing.

Ask for something from you, and that is what you may give, but only something from you.

Those in need of this or that may well get this or that, but only this or that in your time and in your way.

But those who seek you, who may stumble in their asking, who may not know how to ask you for you, you who are above all gifts and cravings of this world, these you will bless beyond those who ask merely for your blessing, beyond those who only want something from you.

Until we learn to ask you for you, for your presence, your Spirit, your love, sufficient beyond our imaginings, we will not understand what is truly important, what our deepest need is finally about, what your blessing can really mean.

You are so gentle, so patient, O God; you will give us, when you choose, only what we ask for, but no more—unless in your grace you choose to lead us beyond ourselves.

You are yourself the more so few know or yet desire to ask for.

When ready, go back and meditate on Psalm 73:25–26: "Whom have I in heaven but you? And there is nothing on earth that I desire other than you. My flesh and my heart may fail, but God is the strength of my heart and my portion forever." Are you now seeking God for God, or for what God can do for you? God will not correct you for asking for things of or from God; accept being where you are, while you are there. God surely does. Look forward to the day when you truly seek God for God, and find in God the one true treasure of the heart.

THE END OF PRAYER

WHAT IS THE ULTIMATE end of prayer? By that I mean both the ultimate goal of prayer, what the heart seeks, and also the ultimate ending of prayer as an exercise we do, as something driven by our hearts for what we seek, but do not yet have. While it will not likely happen during our lifetime, we can nevertheless get intimations of what is coming. Here is my prayer to God:

The end of prayer is abiding in you.

How significant that "end" means both cessation and goal.

Is it any longer prayer when I rest in you; is it still asking when I receive you?

Do hunger and thirst remain once you satisfy me with yourself?

Prayer involves motion and direction; prayer seeks communication, either from you or me—or both.

Prayer is an actional working; but abiding in you is a stilled being.

The former seeks an audience, the latter has more than a mere hearing; it delights in having your being, and remaining for a time beyond time in you and with you.

When you and I are one there is nothing left to do or seek.

Time ceases as duration expands to heights and depths and breadths not to be grasped, which grasp us in measureless totality.

Abiding then is something beyond prayer, greater than the exchanges of communication, where there remains separation as well as connection, either-or as well as both-and.

Abiding means co-union, a communion greater than an "ephemeral I" seeking dialogue with the "eternal you"; now there is purely an "endless we."

When abiding together with you, I am doing nothing; I just am, with and in you.

My single "task" is to attend with my whole being, my whole heart, to you and your Spirit-love silently surrounding and filling me.

I hold nothing of me back or apart or at any distance from you.

I am all in to your all in all.

This ecstatic moment is when you actually enter the oceanic waters of God, after you have passed through whatever is yet to come. Once you have entered into mystical prayer, once you have encountered, been touched by God, by your now forever beloved, the knowledge will also be given to you that there is more to the story of your life and its final fulfillment than what can be accomplished in this brief span of preparation. The end of your prayer journey here is but the beginning of your blessed union there.

AFTERWORD

CORPORATE PRAYER

THE PRAYERS OFFERED IN this book can be prayed in small groups as well as alone. That is, these prayers are for the body of Christ, the church, both for individual members and for the whole body itself. It is of the utmost significance that in the Bible, the giving of the Holy Spirit, came when the followers of Jesus were gathered together. First, in John 20:20–21, the resurrected Jesus breathed the Holy Spirit onto his gathered disciples. Second, in Acts 2:1–4, the Holy Spirit rained down upon a greater number of gathered disciples, in a most dramatic fashion.

Twenty centuries later, I discovered the significance of the gathered body of Christ when the Holy Spirit came down upon me during the initial meeting of a small prayer group formed in order to seek the "baptism of the Holy Spirit." The truth is, *corporate prayer revives and strengthens personal prayer*. And personal prayer grounds and intensifies corporate prayer. The two fundamental modes of prayer support each other.

One well-founded way of proceeding in small groups is through a corporate "Praying the Scriptures" (*Lectio Divina*). It is an effective process, which usually lasts about thirty minutes:

1. The Scripture passage is read silently. Silence follows, as the passage is taken in.

2. One person recites the passage, followed by silence.

3. After a few minutes, another person reads aloud the same passage, followed by silence.

4. Then the four questions are slowly raised, each by a different person, if there are sufficient member. Verbal responses by the members are lifted up for each question.

   1. What does the passage say?

   2. What does the passage say to you?

3. What do you want to say to God?

4. What is God saying to you?

5. Finally, what follows is a discussion of what just transpired. What did the members get out of the process? This could be followed by silent prayer, either centering or abiding prayer. It could last another twenty to thirty minutes. At this point, each member would be praying on their own, though still together, at the same place and time. When we gather together in Christ's name, Jesus said, "I am there among them" (Matt 18:20).

These four questions can be raised and discussed in a prayer group for virtually every prayer offered in this book. Thus, the book can be of real value for small groups.

One last reminder: where is the kingdom of God? Here is Jesus' definitive answer:

> Once Jesus was asked by the Pharisees when the kingdom of God was coming, and he answered, "The kingdom of God is not coming with things that can be observed; nor will they say, 'Look, here it is!' or 'There it is!' For, in fact, the kingdom of God is among you" (Luke 17:20–21).

As noted earlier, the Greek preposition that is translated as "among" is *entos*. It means both "within" and "between" or "among." This indicates that God's reign is already here, though invisible; it is *between and within* us. Hence, corporate prayer will empower private prayer, as the water of the Spirit will overfill vessels of the individuals gathered together in prayer. A satisfying prayer life includes both individual and corporate prayer.

PRAYER PERSEVERANCE AND GUIDANCE

> "Beloved, I do not consider that I have made it my own; but this one thing I do: forgetting what lies behind and straining forward to what lies ahead, I press on toward the goal for the prize of the heavenly call of God in Christ Jesus." (Phil 3:13)

> "Therefore, since we are surrounded by so great a cloud of witnesses, let us also lay aside every weight and the sin that clings so closely, and let us run with perseverance the race that is set before us, looking to Jesus the pioneer and perfecter of our faith, who for the sake of the joy that was set before him endured the cross, disregarding its shame, and has taken his seat at the right hand of the throne of God. Consider him who endured such hostility against himself from sinners, so that you may not grow weary or lose heart." (Heb 12:1–3)

TO CONTINUE YOUR PRAYER journey all the way to its end in God will require faith and perseverance, both of which God will grant you, if you are willing to receive them. I hope that your deepest desire is to know God directly, and to enter into a kind of prayer dialogue that once begun will have no end. If so, rest assured that God will teach you how to pray (Rom 8:26–28). And your heart will direct you arrow-like toward God.

It is imperative that you also seek *companions* on your journey to God, among both the living and those who have entered the "cloud of witnesses." Seek multiple sources of insight and inspiration, beginning with the Scriptures. Then read and interact spiritually with those contemplatives who have preceded you. They will be invaluable *models* and *mentors* for the ways of and life with God. The medieval mystic saints offer this to me; Bernard of Clairvaux (1090–1153) above all, has been my model and mentor in the ways of life with Christ. This great spiritual master gave me a vision of the entire journey that even now continues to prove its accuracy, a bit like Einstein's vision of the nature of the universe.

I offer my story in briefest terms. As already indicated in the Preface, I first encountered God during a prayer meeting in the basement of a Catholic church on Friday, November 17, 1967. I received the "baptism of the Holy Spirit" at what turned out to be the beginning of the Catholic Charismatic Renewal. Three days after that, while "praying in the Spirit," God addressed me for the very first time. In a "voiceless echo," a voice said, "Move on, there is more." Rather than scare me, it intrigued me. I wanted to know what else God had in mind.

A month later, during my evening prayer, I discovered what God had for me next. It felt as if my soul was suddenly, yet ever so gently, lifted slightly up off my bed and ushered into a "temple invisible," which was more intensely real than this world, and strangely not of it. There I met God the "eternal you" in an unexpected intimacy completely beyond words. Thus began a nearly five-year mystical period when I was granted permission to enter that holy space most every time I prayed. During the last four of those mystical years, I was an assistant professor of psychology at Iowa Wesleyan College in Mt. Pleasant, Iowa. Thus, I was a psychologist by day and a mystic by night. I persevered in this evolving prayer life, as the mysteries of God only deepened. The major element that I became acutely aware of was that my feelings toward God were becoming increasingly romantic. I found myself seeking God as my beloved, as my desired spouse in addition to an honored Father. This was most troubling. Was I supposed to feel this way?

Through a decisive chain of events, including my heart's desire, I left teaching to go into pastoral ministry. Shortly before entering the ministry in the United Methodist Church, however, the previous ready access to the temple invisible shut completely. After a priceless romantic prayer of pure togetherness, in May 1972 came the unexpected, heart-piercing words from God: "It will not always be like this." Talk about an understatement! I would beg God for years for a return to those salad days of spiritual union, but to no avail. For the longest time, I feared that I had done, or not done, something that prompted the Lord of life to cut me off. But no answer or return to the former intimacy ever came about. It would be thirty-one years before I finally found out what plan God had for my destiny. Stubborn person that I am, I long resisted a heart-to-heart union with Jesus Christ. (I tell the story about this in my book, *The Heart of Jesus and the Coming Relationship*.)

Fortunately, once in seminary, I finally got to study the medieval mystic saints. To my grateful amazement, I discovered where I truly belonged. Beginning with Saint Bernard of Clairvaux, who became my patron saint, these great mystics confirmed what I had gone through, and the previously unknown fact, which these mystics knew and lived, that our desire for God, paralleling God's even greater desire for us, was romantic in nature, destined for a spiritual marriage-like union with God. Prior to that welcome discovery, I feared that there was something wrong with me. But these mystic leaders of the church universal confirmed that what I was desiring was of and from God. It turned out that God had secretly implanted my desire for God; it was God's gift of grace and an invitation for intimacy. Centuries before me, God had done in them what God was doing in me. I was not the first to travel down this singular yet boundless path, which is both of and to God.

To be clear: these medieval mystics, such as Saints Catherine of Siena, John of the Cross, and Theresa of Avila, *did not plant the desire for God in me, or tell me exactly how to pray.* Rather, they *confirmed* what I had already learned through years of prayer being the center of my daily life. And through their own prayer lives, they served as *vital models and mentors* of those who not only sought God with their whole hearts, but who found what I was seeking: direct connection to, and union with, God. Yet it remains the Holy Spirit, the inner advocate sent by Jesus Christ, who *teaches* how to pray directly. Jesus said, "I still have many things to say to you, but you cannot bear them now. When the Spirit of truth comes, he will guide you into all the truth; for he will not speak on his own, but will speak whatever he hears, and he will declare to you the things that are to come" (John 16:12–13).

About this, Paul said: "Likewise the Spirit helps us in our weakness; for we do not know how to pray as we ought, but that very Spirit intercedes with sighs too deep for words. And God, who searches the heart, knows what is the mind of the Spirit, because the Spirit intercedes for the saints according to the will of God" (Rom 8:26–27).

In sum, the mystics who preceded you, together with living contemplatives, clergy, and spiritually mature friends, will *confirm* your heart-led path to union with God as your ultimate beloved. And they will hopefully *model* and *mentor* you along your prayer journey. But note carefully: it is God, and God alone, who is at work within you (Phil 2:13), and who will *teach* you and *guide your heart* to your destined meeting with, and eternal life in, God. Trust that and persevere in prayer. Do so and your end in God is assured.

CPSIA information can be obtained
at www.ICGtesting.com
Printed in the USA
BVHW071836130123
656260BV00008B/848